AF580329

APPLES OF GOLD

A Handbook For
Christian Elementary Teachers

By

Jean Evans & June Hornsby

Illustrations By

Mona Hsu

MASTER BOOK PUBLISHERS
SAN DIEGO, CALIFORNIA 92115

APPLES OF GOLD

MASTER BOOK PUBLISHERS, A Division of CLP
P. O. Box 15908
San Diego, California 92115

Library of Congress Catalog Card Number 84-61281
ISBN 0-89051-106-3

Cataloging in Publication Data

Hornsby, June, 1941-
Apples of gold; a handbook for Christian elementary teachers, by Dr. June Hornsby and Jean Evans, illustrated by Mona Hsu.

1. Elementary school teaching—Handbooks, manuals, etc. 2. Christian education. I. Evans, Jean, 1941- joint author. II. Title. III. Title: A handbook for Christian elementary teachers.

372.13

ISBN 0-89051-106-3 84-61281

Printed in the United States of America

Acknowledgments

Our heartfelt thanks and love are expressed to our friends and family who helped with completing this project:

To our editors, our husbands, Wayne Evans and Ben Hornsby.

To our talented artist, Mona Hsu.

To our typist and psychologist, Dianne Stark, for her labor of love.

And, finally, to George Hillestad who had enough faith in us to publish our book.

Dedication

TO OUR FAMILY

Preface

The primary purpose in writing this book is to present practical information to the beginning Christian teacher. Through the integration of Scripture and by sharing our experiences in the teaching profession, we seek to motivate sound, workable solutions to some of the more significant challenges of the elementary classroom.

There are some skills that cannot be learned from a book. In almost any profession you must practice and experience the task that you have studied. There are few professionals who feel confident about their skills until they have practiced them. However, it is our desire to give some advice and instruction that can be useful to you as you begin your teaching experience. Hopefully, we can aid you in avoiding some potential pitfalls.

Our prayer is that our words may be "fitly spoken" and that they will be our "apples of gold in pictures of silver" to you, the future teachers of our children (Proverbs 25:11).

Jean Evans
June Hornsby

About The Authors

The authors are twins. Their collective experience as teachers totals twenty-five years and includes elementary, junior high, and college levels of instruction. They are both married to ministers, and they both graduated from Mississippi College, a private denominational college in Clinton, Mississippi.

Jean Evans received her M.S. from the University of Southern Mississippi and currently teaches reading to junior high students in Rochester, Minnesota. She has taught on the elementary level in Mississippi, Florida, Louisiana, and Georgia.

June Hornsby has her M.S. and Ed.D. degrees from the University of Southern Mississippi. She has taught elementary students in Mississippi, Montana, and Louisiana. Currently she is Associate Professor of Education at Christian Heritage College in El Cajon, California. She supervises the elementary student teachers.

The illustrator, Mona Hsu, is from Taiwan. She has her M.A.L.S. from the University of Michigan and her B.F.A. from Cleveland Institute of Art. She worked as an artist at Moody Bible Institute and as a cataloguer at Miami University. Currently she is a cataloguer in the library at Christian Heritage College.

Contents

1. Teaching, The Task 15
2. Resumés, Applications, and Interviews 21
3. Lesson Planning 29
4. Classroom Management 37
5. Discipline Suggestions 41
6. Room Appearance and Bulletin Boards 45
7. Motivating Students 59
8. Diagnosing Student Needs 63
9. Teaching Slow Learners 69
10. Parent-Teacher Conferences 73
11. Interpersonal Relationships 77
12. Substituting 81
13. Professional Growth 87
14. Teacher Feedback 91
15. Teachers Who Burn Out 95
16. Joyful Teaching 101

Appendix 103

Bibliography 121

Chapter One

Teaching, The Task

Each year children enter your class and each one is an individual. In His great wisdom as the Master Designer, God has made each person unique. There have never been two of us exactly alike since time began. Even identical twins have different fingerprints. What a wonderful Creator God we serve!

You, as the teacher, must take the child—where he is presently—and as he grows in stature, help him to mature in wisdom and in favor with God and man, as well. There are teachers who complain about the students. They may think that the teacher last year did not prepare them adequately, or that the parents did not use biblical principles in rearing the child. Everyone is born with certain characteristics and personality possibilities. Both a child's environment and his heredity determine the product that you receive in your classroom. Only Christ can make major changes as a life is committed totally to Him (John 1:12; II Corinthians 5:17).

Teachers are to give guidance to the children and to pray for them. Accepting the child as he is—with all his weaknesses and strengths—is quite important. Assume the challenge of the task, roll up your sleeves, and tackle the job. "And he gave some. . .teachers, for the perfecting of the saints, for the work of the ministry, for the edifying of the body of Christ" (Ephesians 4:11).

The task of a teacher may seem impossible. You are expected to shepherd a child—on his own level and at his own pace—to relative competence in every subject and to keep proper records of it all. You are expected to challenge him, inspire him, and equip him with the necessary basic skills, to accomplish this task perhaps with limited funds and facilities, and to do it all with *love*. How can a teacher face such a difficult task? Only with God are all things possible! (Matthew 19:26).

The following suggestions have served experienced teachers well in organizing for the task of teaching.

1. GROUP THE STUDENTS

Where do you begin with thirty (plus) students who all seem to be on different levels of learning in different subjects? The challenge is to teach all of them all of the skills they need for successful completion of the grade level to which you are assigned. Even after four or five years of training to teach, you still may find it difficult to know where to begin—exactly where is "square one"?

Obviously, the *ideal* way to accomplish the task of teaching each child is to have one teacher per child. That is not feasible, of course, for many reasons. Therefore, "grouping" may be used to teach students who have similar needs.

For example, the first step in grouping for reading would be to evaluate the student's performance in order to determine which students belong together. The grade level you are teaching determines the type of evaluation you should. There are many published tests available. Two examples are: (1) Woodcock Reading Mastery Test (K-12), American Guidance Service, Publisher Building, Circle Pines, Minnesota 55014; and (2) Sucher-Allred Reading Placement Inventory, The Economy Company, Box 25308, Oklahoma City, Oklahoma 73125.

You can devise your own tests, however, by simply utilizing letters of the alphabet, blends, and other phonetic elements which you feel are applicable to your grade level. Then type or copy paragraphs from several different level readers, with accompanying comprehension questions. Have each child come to your desk, give the sounds, read, and answer the questions orally. The levels of reading are as follows:

Independent level—recognizes 99% of the words and answers 90% of the comprehension questions correctly;

Instructional level—recognizes 95% of the words and answers 70% of the comprehension questions correctly;

Frustration level—recognizes fewer than 90% of the words and answers fewer than 50% of the comprehension questions correctly.

Some teachers (and publishing companies) prefer instructing their classes in reading as a whole group in the mornings. They can use this time to work on phonics instruction or sight-words lists. Then in the afternoon, the class works in groups. One group reads to the teacher, another group writes or copies from the board, and a third group does an activity that may include art, listening to recordings, reinforcement sheets, or drills. Each group moves to another activity every fifteen to twenty minutes as you ring a bell, call time, or clap.

Grouping can be utilized successfully in other subjects also. For example, introduce a math concept such as long division. Teach several days and then give problems to the students. Group them according to the number they worked correctly. The students who missed 0 - 1 are in the first group; those who missed 2 - 3 are in group two; those who missed 4 - 5 are in group three. For three days work with them in these groups. Challenge the first group with added concepts or let them tutor those in group two. The third group will work with the teacher at the board. Then, give an additional five problems to all students and regroup. It is exciting!

English can be grouped into two sections. Those who can write sentences using correct verbs, quotations marks, capital letters, etc., or correctly write letters comprise Section I. Section I can work independently while you work with those who need further instruction (Section II).

Remember to keep the groups or sections fluid and flexible so that when concepts are mastered, the child can slip easily into another group. If you have parents or volunteers in your classroom, they can be assigned to work with groups.

Grouping may not be the ideal, but it can provide the teacher with a workable solution to many problems. An added dimension of grouping is that students must work together and can be reminded that we are to love and serve each other (I John 4:7 and Matthew 12:31).

2. USE YOUR GIFTS

God made each of us like Him in that we are created in His image (Genesis 1:27). Yet individuals are given different gifts (I Corinthians 4:14), "Now there are diversities of gifts, but the same spirit."

There are many different methods or techniques to use in teaching. Something that may work for one teacher may not work for another. You cannot be just like another teacher. We should not have as our objective to be just like the teacher next door, but to be like the Master Teacher, Jesus.

Use your gifts and abilities in teaching. If you really enjoy science, then teach your students to enjoy it. Go on field trips, plan experiments, or find media resources about the subject. Have plants growing and sprouting all over the room. Get excited about it and be a fantastic science teacher! You may want to share your excitement with another teacher in the school by letting another class take advantage of a particular lesson or experiment. Then the other teacher can share expertise in his particular area with your class.

If social studies is your area of high interest, then delve into the subject with all your energies. Let the children make murals, maps, clay communities, or cardboard villages. Let a missionary speak to the class about living in another culture.

Math can be fun using relays for drills and teams at board work. Spelling drills can be made fun by using spelldowns, writing words and tracing over them with different colors to make a design, by using coils of clay to write a word, by using yarn and glue to correlate spelling and art, or by playing "concentration" with the words on cards.

Language lessons can be enlivened by writing or copying sentences using the children's names. Students can write to pen pals in a neighboring school, and plans can be made for the classes to meet one another for a reading activity. Let the older students tutor younger students, or listen to the kindergarten group, or read a story to them. Put life into subjects that could become paper and pencil routines.

Art, music, or physical education activities really excite some teachers and have the opposite effect on others. Maximize your gifts in the areas you really enjoy and do not feel guilty about not really enjoying the subject areas which the teacher next door enjoys. If you will share with each other, both you and your classes will benefit from it.

3. PARENTS AND HOMEWORK

The work that is sent home for the students to do should have been *taught* in class. Some types of drill assignments that are acceptable homework may include: spelling words, facts to be memorized in math, recopying work, or reading library books. Parents should not be expected to teach new concepts. They may have been taught steps to the solution of a question or problem which are different from the ones you are teaching. The child could become more confused in the process. You should also be aware of the amount of time it will take the students to complete the assignments. Some teachers send work home because it was not completed in class. Sometimes the amount of homework needs to be adjusted for slow learners. Some primary teachers send home a weekly sheet that lists homework assignments for each night. As the child gets older, however, fewer announcements of this type need to be sent home. The student should begin to accept responsibility as soon as possible. Be sure that *you* are doing the job of *teaching* at school, and that you do not expect the parents to do it; however, they should be well-informed as to the purpose of the assignments.

4. REDEEM THE TIME

Have you ever complained that there were only five minutes left and nothing could be accomplished in that little time? Or have you ever noticed a class that loses ten to fifteen minutes preparing for the next subject?

Wasting only five minutes a day is wasting twenty-five minutes a week, or one hour and forty minutes a month! Incorporate a drill on math facts, spelling drills, or learning words to a song in those five-minute spaces. There are many times when only five minutes are left; five minutes before lunch, before lining up to go home, after a special program, or before beginning the next lesson. Be a good steward—use every minute.

5. TEACHING THE EXTRAS

Teaching objectives should include more than the cognitive or knowledge domain. The psychomotor and affective aspects of learning should also be included. Psychomotor learning includes those activities which use the muscles, such as writing, cutting and pasting, or using the hands and feet. The affective domain includes the attitude and feelings of the student. It includes Christian characteristics that make us more like the Master Teacher.

Teach the children in your class to:

a. Care

(Proverbs 18:24: "A man that hath friends must show himself friendly: and there is a friend that sticketh closer than a brother.")

- for each other
- for the school and personnel
- for learning

b. Observe

(II Timothy 4:5a: "But watch thou in all things. . . .")

- needs of others
- nature and the world around them
- current events

c. Think

(Proverbs 1:5: "A wise man will hear, and will increase learning; and a man of understanding shall attain unto wise counsels."

- for themselves
- for solutions

d. Understand

(Romans 12:15: "Be of the same mind one toward another. Mind not high things, but condescend to men of low estate. Be not wise in your own conceits.")

- others and their problems
- parents and their stresses
- problems in our country and world

d. Share

(II Corinthians 9:7: "Every man according as he purposeth in his heart, so let him give; not grudgingly, or of necessity: for God loveth a cheerful giver.")

- their ideas and dreams
- their knowledge
- their equipment and belongings

e. Grow

(Luke 2:52: "And Jesus increased in wisdom and stature, and in favor with God and man.")

- toward maturity
- toward accepting themselves
- toward Christ-likeness

6. PREPARE TO WORK

In order to keep up with thirty "live wires," the teacher will have to stay plugged in to the Rock of all ages! ("The Lord is my rock, and my fortress, and my deliverer; my God, my strength, in whom I will trust; my buckler, and the horn of my salvation, and my high tower" Psalm 18:2.) When you feel drained at the end of the day, it probably is not because of the physical work, but because of the stresses, problems, and responsibilities you have faced. The teacher is "on stage" and "at attention" every minute throughout the school day. Remember the source of your strength and claim the biblical promises continually.

Attack the task of teaching as if you were dependent upon the results for your very survival. Then you will know that you have given your best. God rewards those who are faithful and who use their gifts and talents wisely (Matthew 25:21).

Chapter Two

Resumés, Applications, and Interviews

When you begin to look for a teaching position, you will need to prepare a resumé to send to prospective employers. You also may be requested to attend an interview for the job. There are tips and suggestions that will aid you in your attempt to present yourself positively to those who will be evaluating you. It is important to be yourself, not pretending to be anyone else, and to be confident, yet humble. The best advice to remember is found in the scriptures: "Pride goeth before destruction and a haughty spirit before a fall" (Proverbs 16:18).

1. RESUMÉS AND APPLICATIONS

The etymology of "resumé" is French and means "summary." It is a short account of one's career and qualifications. As you write it, remember that you are presenting a mental picture of yourself. Use a good quality grade of paper, have the best typing job possible, and make sure the words are all spelled correctly. If a principal has several candidates to consider for one position, you can be sure that the resumé/application with misspelled words will go to the bottom of the pile.

There are several acceptable styles for a resumé, however, the following information is generally included:

Name Address Phone Number Date of Birth Marital Status	Home address (or permanent address) Phone number	Picture, if desired

State your employment objective, that is, the kind of job you are seeking. List in order of your preference.

EDUCATION

List schools beginning with the first degree received.	In this column list your degrees and the year you received them. High School degrees may be omitted.

WORK EXPERIENCE

List the name and the address of places where you have worked.	List the dates and your position in each employment, beginning with the earliest ones.

EXPERIENCE WITH CHILDREN

Give the name of the club, school, choir, class, or camp, etc., in which you worked.	State the position in which you worked.

(STUDENT) TEACHING EXPERIENCE

If this is your first teaching position, you may give your student teaching experience. If you have taught before, list the schools here beginning with the earliest experience.

INTERESTS

Most schools will expect you to involve yourself with extracurricular activities. Your interest areas will alert them to the areas in which you could be competent. List things such as drama, sewing, photography, sports, singing, playing an instrument, art, writing, and any foreign language knowledge.

REFERENCES

Give the names, positions, and addresses of three people who can recommend you for teaching. When possible, obtain permission from the persons you list as references.

Most colleges have a placement service for their graduates. If your college provides this service, you do not need to list any references in the resumé since your placement folder will contain letters of reference, and prospective employers may request that information from the college.

When possible, include all of the information listed above on one sheet. If you need two pages, you should use the back since two sheets could be easily separated and misplaced.

2. APPLICATIONS

When the resumé has been completed, send it along with a cover letter in which you personalize your request for employment. For example, you would write a letter, using a business format, to the District Office stating that you would like to apply for a teaching position. State that you are including a resumé and that you would like them to send you an application. Include in your letter why you desire to work in their school district.

If they are interested, they will send an application which you should complete and return promptly. If you do not type your application, use black ink. Do not change ink colors throughout the process. This may sound detailed, but principals have been known to throw away those applications that violate any of the rules presented above. Most principals also prefer to have a picture attached, especially if there is a space reserved for it. By paying attention to the details, you are giving them two messages: (1) whether or not you are serious about the job; and (2) an idea about how you might complete any job that may be assigned to you. As has been mentioned before, the scriptures inform us about how we should conduct our business: "Let all things be done decently and in order" (I Corinthians 14:40).

3. INTERVIEWS

Usually the candidates for a teaching position are screened down to two or three persons from written applications. In a large school district, the applications are filed at the district office and are available to all of the principals in the district. If your application is chosen, you are usually contacted for an interview. You may be interviewed by the principal or by a group which may include board members and/or other teachers.

Allow plenty of time to get to the interview so that you will not have to rush, be hassled, or wonder if your head is screwed on straight. By the same token, do not arrive so early that you have a great deal of time on your hands after you arrive to sit around and get nervous. Time your arrival carefully.

a. Be Prepared

Before going to an interview, pray that God will give you a calm spirit and that His will may be done. Remember II Timothy 1:7 and claim one of God's promises: "For God hath not given us the spirit of fear; but of power and of love, and of a sound mind." Then you can organize your thoughts and provide the information asked of you to the very best of your ability.

You probably will have from twenty minutes to an hour to convince the person(s) conducting the interview that you are the right choice for the job. Find out some things about the school or district. Be knowledgeable about their needs and goals. Use your conversation, your manner, and your enthusiasm to impress upon them the fact that you would be the best candidate for the vacant position. Remain humble, but you may have to "toot your own horn" to inform them of your successful past experiences.

Being able to anticipate questions that may be asked can help you prepare answers that you would like to give. The following list includes some questions that might be included in your interview:

1. Tell us about yourself.
2. What factors led you to decide to become a teacher?
3. What age child do you prefer to work with and why?
4. How do you feel about discipline?
5. How would you handle disruptive behavior?
6. Tell how you would group a room of children for reading.
7. In your opinion, what makes a good teacher?
8. How would you set up your classroom for your particular subject area?
9. What is the name of a reading series you could use?
10. What do you enjoy most about teaching?
11. Generally, what is your philosophy of education?
12. How would you motivate your students?
13. Tell what I might see if I entered your classroom.
14. Why do you want to teach with us?
15. How would you go about teaching a skill or concept?
16. Do you work well with others? Give examples.
17. What experiences have you had in working with students?
18. Do you feel that student teaching has prepared you for teaching? (Why/why not?)
19. What strengths and weaknesses do you think you bring to the classroom?
20. How do you view those who are in authority over you?

b. Be Well-dressed

You have only one chance to give a first impression. You will need to plan to make it a good one. We like to think that others will appreciate us for who we are instead of how we look, but that usually takes time. During an interview you have an hour or less to make a lasting impression. When God told

Samuel to go anoint a king after Saul's death, Samuel felt certain that one of Jesse's older sons would be chosen. However, God told him, "Look not on his countenance, or on the height of his stature; because I have refused him: for the Lord seeth not as man seeth; for man looketh on the outward appearance, but the Lord looketh on the heart" (I Samuel 16:7). God does see the most important part of us, our soul and heart, but man cannot. We tend to rely on the outward appearance, because that is all we can see.

Wear clothes that are comfortable but nice. Save the tennis clothes and blue jeans for sports or informal situations. On the other hand, be careful not to overdress. A suit or a sports jacker is appropriate, with jewelry and make-up (for women) in moderation. The darker the colors worn, the more authoritative you will appear. A contrasting blouse or shirt would also appear professional. Wear church-type clothes rather than evening attire. If you are interested in reading further about professional dress, the following books are suggested:

Color Me Beautiful, by Carl Jackson (Washington: Acropolis Books, 1980).
Dress For Success, by John Malloy (New York: P. H. Wyden, 1975).
Dress With Style, by Joann Wallace (New Jersey: Fleming Revell Company, 1983).
Looking Terrific, by Emily Cho and Linda Grover (New York: Ballantine Books, 1978).

Joann Wallace's book is written from a Christian's perspective.

Be neat. Shine your shoes and have your hair clean and shining. Never waltz in chewing gum. Have your mouth clear for intelligent conversation.

Wear a smile and be glad you are there. If smiling is not part of your present personality, then practice rejoicing always as we are admonished to do in Philippians 4:4, "Rejoice in the Lord alway: and again I say , Rejoice," and also I Thessalonians 5:16, "Rejoice evermore." Try it—it works! The outside of you will show how the inside feels. When you are ready to go, stand in front of a full-length mirror and ask yourself if the overall impression you see is the picture you want to portray. Then go with confidence.

c. Be Correct

The English language is complicated. However, you as a professional should have practiced enough to be able to speak using correct grammar. School administrators want you to have a good command of the King's English.

Use your oral communication skills to your advantage. Answer the questions as well as you can. Be concise and to the point. If you have done anything that you believe would be worth noting, you can insert it appropriately somewhere in the conversation. Do not ramble on and on. Do not detract from what you are saying by the way you are saying it. Speak correctly.

d. Be Natural

School personnel want teachers who like children. They are hunting someone who wants to teach, not someone who is just looking for a job. Show by your body language, voice tone, questions, and answers that you are genuinely interested in children. Be able to communicate this interest to those with whom you talk, and they will know that you would communicate the same feelings to your fellow teachers and school children.

Be excited about the prospects of seeing the school plant where you might work. Ask some questions about how their system works. Principals always feel that they have something good to offer a teacher, and they are happy to show off their facilities. Be interested. If you can be "bubbly" about anything, now would be a good time to produce a few bubbles. The feeling you should have at the moment should be similar to the feeling of a swimmer looking at a pool, a skater looking at ice, or a baker looking at rising dough. You want to get in there and do your best. Your eagerness to be involved will be evident. The interviewer(s) will notice. You will not be able to fake your way through an interview. Just make sure that your love for God, for your profession, and for the children with whom you will work shines through. There are countless scriptures in the Bible dealing with the subject of love. It is the subject of the first two commandments and the theme of many passages. We are reminded many times that if we know God, if we want to know we are Christians, and if we want the world to know we are Christians, then we are to LOVE (I John 3:14; I John 4, and I Corinthians 13).

e. Be Positive

An interview is not a good place to air all your grievances against the educational system. If there is anything worth remembering in this book, it is the advice to be positive. Be positive in all that you do. Practice looking on the bright side. Anyone can find fault and complain, but if you want the job, refrain from negative comments about anything. If you are negative, you may well destroy the positive impression you have achieved to this point. Nobody likes to have a whining, complaining, "something-is-always-wrong" person on his staff, and you will not be there either if you let negativism creep into your discussion. If you have disliked many of the people with whom you have worked in the past, you probably won't like these people either. They are listening to hear if you work well with others or if you are always clashing.

If the principal likes your interview, he will probably have a discussion with your last supervisor. This discussion will be the final factor in his decision. He has already read your college transcript, comments from your supervising teacher, student teaching records, and (if you have already been teaching) recommendations from other principals. The principal has decided that you came across favorably in your interview. Hopefully, when he calls your last supervisor, he will get a good report. That is why it is necessary, even though you might disagree with former principals or policies, to leave a job with a good record. Never burn the bridges behind you because you will have to walk back over them. Your record stays with you for life, and you can never go back and change the record. It stands as it was recorded. Make it a good one and one that you would be proud for anyone to examine. Always do your best. Even though there may be disagreements or disappointments, never leave a place angry, even if it depends solely upon you to straighten it out. Several verses that speak about anger are Proverbs 16:32 ("He that is slow to anger is better than the mighty; and he that ruleth his spirit than he that taketh a city") and Proverbs 29:22 ("An angry man stirreth up strife, and a furious man aboundeth in transgression.") Another verse in Proverbs tells us how important it is to have a good reputation: "A good name is rather to be chosen than great riches, and loving favour than silver and gold" (Proverbs 22:1).

Any or all of the steps included in this chapter about obtaining a job may be omitted in certain circumstances. Some students are hired where they student teach and may not go through any formal application procedures.

Sometimes you may obtain an application and will not need a resumé at all. You may use the information included in this chapter as the need arises.

Chapter Three

Lesson Planning

Teaching includes a great deal of planning. Schools generally require some type of written plans from the teacher so that a substitute may continue your instruction if you have to be absent, so that you will be organized and know the purposes, directions, and materials needed for daily lessons, and so that the principal can be knowledgeable about your instruction. You will probably be given directions from the principal about what is expected in this area. You need to understand his expectations and carry them out to the best of your ability (Col. 3:23).

Some of the aspects that you need to think through about lesson planning are listed and discussed below:

1. THE LONG FORM

Education majors usually learn how to fill out and follow a long form for their lesson planning. A sample copy is shown in Figure 1. Column 1 shows the minutes you intend to spend on each aspect of the lesson. Column 2 includes the behavioral objectives. Each objective should be written so that the behavior can be observed or measured. An example would be, "Each student (by the end of the lesson) will be able to write five exclamatory sentences." Verbs such as "appreciate" or "understand" should be used for broad goals and not for specific objectives since these descriptive terms cannot be measured. The number of objectives will vary according to the time alloted for the total lesson and according to the content of the subject.

The third column under "Anticipatory Set" includes the following:

a. Rationale

You have a reason for presenting the lesson. You state it such as, "So that the students will be able to recognize and write correct and complete sentences."

b. Motivation

Think about how you can make the lesson interesting and stimulating. For

Lesson Plan Form

Student Teacher's Name ________________ Subject ____________ Grade ______ Date ____

Lesson Topic ____

Timing	Behavioral Objective(s)	Anticipatory Set	Teacher Activities and Materials Needed	Student Activities	Evaluation
		Rationale: Motivation: Provision for Transfer:			

Scriptural Integration (when applicable):

Comments:

Figure 1.

some lessons it might include media—a picture, slide presentation, film, or bulletin board display. For other lessons it might be questions you would ask, a discussion, a riddle, a song, a poem, or an announcement by someone outside the classroom. Motivation for the lesson might also include telling them about incentives, such as privileges, awards, or recognition for completing the assignment correctly.

c. Provision for Transfer

One purpose for teaching a lesson is that the students will be able to use that information in real life. You have to think through how you can detect whether or not they have grasped the concepts for their own use. For example, after studying the mechanics for writing a business letter, you may give the students an assignment to write one and request that they include certain information; or you may listen to them read after having explained a certain aspect of phonics or word analysis.

d. Teacher Activities and Materials Needed

Under this topic you may include any notes about the content of the lesson that you need to remember and the specific materials that you may need to have available. Many lessons will only require a textbook, a chalkboard, and/or work sheets. However, if you are giving a demonstration or if some type of media is required, those materials are listed in this column.

e. Student Activities

Picture in your mind the steps through which you would like the students to go during the lesson. List the steps in the fifth column. The number of student activities will vary greatly with the age of the students, your purposes or objectives for the lesson, and the time allotted.

f. Evaluation

There are other ways to evaluate students than to give a test. In the sixth column you summarize the various activities included and determine which ones will give you an evaluation of their knowledge about the concepts presented. Your observation may be one way to evaluate them. Keen teacher observation can give a valid evaluation of student knowledge. This may include anything from scanning around the room to observe student behavior to pinpointing those needing individual attention.

Evaluation may also include textbook assignments, worksheets, quizzes, exams, homework assignments, workbook pages assigned, oral presentations, or any other observable behavior (such as dramas, etc.). Figures 2 and 3 are examples of lesson plans written by student teachers as they planned for different lessons and levels of instruction.

Figure 2.

Lesson Plan Form

Student Teacher's Name Kristen Maiellaro Subject Language Arts Grade 3 Date 9/10

Lesson Topic Using Complete sentences

Timing	Behavioral Objective(s)	Anticipatory Set	Teacher Activities and Materials Needed	Student Activities	Evaluation
10 min. 15 min.	The student will be able to: 1) State components neccssary to form a complete sentence. 2) Answer questions orally in complete sentences. 3) Create and state a complete sentence. 4) Display a positive attitude towards activity through participation and listening. 5) Demonstrate correct oral speaking.	Rationale: to enable students to use complete sentences and to transfer this knowledge to creative speaking. Motivation: Telling a story on tape and then listening to it. Provision for Transfer: The student will orally give sentences for a story and will write the sentences correctly.	Materials 1) Cassette tape player 2) Cassette tape 3) Chalk board Activities 1) Discuss complete sentences. Write samples on chalkboard. 2) Assist students in choosing a topic for a story. 3) Allow students to practice sentences before recording. 4) Record, then play back tape and evaluate with them.	1) Participate in discussion as lead by teacher. 2) Listen and respond to teacher's questions. 3) Offer sentences for group story. 4) Begin working on homework assignment, if time.	1) Teacher observation 2) Student participation in activities. 3) classwork or homework: write the story in complete sentences that was recorded, or a similar creative story.

Scriptural Integration (when applicable):

Psalms 19:14 "Let the words of my mouth, and the meditation of my heart, be acceptable in thy sight, O Lord, my strength and my redeemer."

Comments:

Figure 3.

Lesson Plan Form

Student Teacher's Name Linda Arford Subject Science Grade 4 Date 5/21

Lesson Topic Properties of water

Timing	Behavioral Objective(s)	Anticipatory Set	Teacher Activities and Materials Needed	Student Activities	Evaluation
5 min. 20-25 min. 10 min	By the end of the lesson the student will be able to: 1) identify the changing properties of water through evaporation, condensation & precipitation. 2) Conduct the experiments on changing properties of water. 3) Support the knowledge gained by discussion. 4) Define key words in a crossword puzzle.	Rationale: To become familiar with the properties of water that are present in everyday life. Motivation: 1) Comic strip on transparency 2) Conduct experiments. Provision for Transfer: 1) Questions to answer about experiments. 2) Oral discussion 3) Defining terms	Activities 1) Read comic from transparency. 2) Discuss vocabulary words. 3) Discuss "H_2O." 4) Prepare students for experiments. 5) Students conduct each experiment by groups. 6) Lead class disussion. Materials 1) Experiments: A. Candle wax, pan hot plate. B. Tea kettle, ice cubes. C. Tea bag, Salt; paper towel.	1) Day before lesson: Compile a list of water functions. 2) Conduct each experiment, if time. 3) Write a short report about each experiment from worksheet. 4) Discuss the experiments with the class.	1) Homework vocabulary words. 2) Observation and reporting of experiments. 3) Observation by teacher.

Scriptural Integration (when applicable): Jesus provides "living Water" to those who ask.

Comments:

2. THE SHORT FORM

Generally, teachers use a lesson plan book that is printed in notebook form and is readily available from teacher supply stores. An example of these forms is found in Figure 4. Different subjects taught are filled in across the top of the page, and plans for each day are written adjacent to that day of the week. Since the spaces are small, abbreviations can be used. However, make certain that a key to the abbreviated forms is included in the planbook. A substitute teacher may not be able to decipher your hieroglyphics well enough to follow through with the intended assignments!

Some principals will require the lesson plan book to be turned in each week and others may want it displayed on your desk so that it may be checked at any time.

Experienced teachers tend to plan for their lessons as they think throughout the day, as they are going about tasks after or before school hours, and even while waiting in gas or grocery lines! There does not seem to be enough time in the school day to get a long form filled out for all seven to ten subjects taught. However, if you have been trained to think through the steps listed on the long form, you will be able to mentally plan through those areas and simply jot down the minimum amount of information on the short form and still be prepared for the lesson.

One very successful Christian teacher said recently that he continues to use the long form for planning his lessons on the high school level. He then evaluates himself and makes a note of it so that the next time he teaches that lesson he can remember what works and what does not. On the elementary level, you might want to fill out the long form for a unit you plan to teach or each time a new concept is introduced to the class.

Whether you use the long form, short form, or a combination of the two will probably depend on your individual situation. The important thing to remember is that planning is vital so that you will be prepared for doing your best—as unto the Lord. Did not our Lord prepare?

(1) He prayed (Matthew 26:36-46). He knew there was a task before Him that was too heavy for Him to bear alone, so He prayed. Many scriptures relate how Jesus prayed before going about a task.

(2) He grouped (Mark 6:39-43). He directed the disciples to seat the multitudes in groups of "hundreds and by fifties."

(3) He planned (Matthew 5:1-2). Before delivering a most impressive and life-changing sermon, He positioned Himself so that all could get the most benefit from His teaching. He began teaching when He was "set."

(4) He prepared (Luke 3:23). Jesus spent a lifetime (over thirty years) of personal preparation before beginning His earthly ministry.

SUBJECT			
MONDAY			
TUESDAY			
WEDNESDAY			
THURSDAY			
FRIDAY			

Figure 4.

Time spent in planning is not time wasted. You will feel prepared and your students will benefit from organized, informative lessons.

Chapter Four

Classroom Management

There are days at school when little or no time is left for the academics. The teacher can become quite frustrated if lesson plans have been carefully written, if he is enthusiastically ready for the day, and then non-teaching essentials fill the time allotted for teaching. As Christian teachers, we must realize that "this is the day which the Lord hath made; we will rejoice and be glad in it" (Psalm 118:24), no matter what the outward circumstances might be! If the day is turned over to the Lord, then we are not responsible for the turn of events—He is.

Every day there are a certain number of non-teaching essentials that must be completed. These may include the role call, announcements from the office, lunch and/or milk monies, and special duties that have been assigned. The teacher should accept these gracefully and gratefully and do them as unto the Lord. Time-saving techniques will be helpful in keeping time spent on the secretarial duties to a minimum. The importance of each non-teaching essential needs to be emphasized. If everything is to be done "decently and in order" (I Cor. 14:40), then we realize how *essential* these *non-essentials* become!

1. BEGINNING OF SCHOOL

Just keep in mind that the remainder of the school year will not be the same as the beginning days. Routine will settle the chaos eventually. There will be lists of names to be made, forms of all kinds to be sent home and filled out, and fees to be collected. The list seems endless, but whatever must be done, do it. Our Lord spoke many times about having a servant's heart (Mark 9:35; Mark 10:44; II Timothy 2:24).

2. COUNTING MONEY

One non-teaching essential that could take a great deal of your time is taking up money for various reasons. You may have lunch money, milk money, picture money, and insurance money to collect during the same week. Organization is essential. A labeled envelope, box, or container is a good starter. If all monies can be taken up at one time, you will be fortunate. However, expect the worse—it may happen! Some parents may send in a brother's amount who is in another class, or one student may forget that he has his money with him until you have already figured your totals. Usually it is easier to collect the money as they bring it. If they keep it, they may lose it on the playground.

3. NEW STUDENTS

There is paperwork involved in enrolling a new student in your class. Book cards have to be signed, dates have to be entered on the cumulative folder, and proper placement of the student into any groups you have will need to be considered.

There may be a tendency to be negative about this added responsibility. Naturally, you will wondering: "Where is he academically?" "Will he be a discipline problem?" "How will he fit into the groups I already have?" The child's feelings should be considered. First of all, he probably left friends and everything familiar when the family moved. Secondly, he probably did not make the decision to move, his parents did. Perhaps the child is frightened, or at least apprehensive, about facing a new school, class, and teacher, not to mention no friends.

How then should you as the teacher react? I John 4:12 states, "And this commandment have we from Him, that he who loveth God love his brother also." If the teacher loves as through God's eyes and heart, then his reaction should be one of love and acceptance. Smile and welcome the new student.

You will have only one chance to make a first impression on the parent(s). You might not see them again during the remainder of the year. To act disgruntled toward the parent(s) or child is not becoming to you as a Christian or to your profession. You never know the potential of a new student, the influence he might have on your class, or the challenge he may present. Be thankful (I Thessalonians 5:18).

4. PARENT-TEACHER ORGANIZATIONS

The parent-teacher organization usually assists the school more than any other group. Attending their meetings is a small contribution you can make. Although sometimes you are required to come back to the school after a long day, and perhaps you have papers yet to grade, the teacher needs to attend joyfully. Rapport with the parents is so necessary. You can understand the children much better if you work with their parents. There may not be many parents, but you can get to know those parents well.

If you find the meetings unproductive, volunteer your class to give a play, to have an art display, or to sing a collection of songs. Go to the meetings with the intentions of learning something and putting something into them. Your responsibility is to be there—go with joy.

5. DUTY

Extra duties are a reality for each teacher. There may be bus duty, recess duty, lunch duty, hall duty, or after school sports to sponsor. There are fire drills and different kinds of catastrophe drills for you to supervise. You may be expected to put hours of work into carnivals or festivals. To be able to come to school and only teach may be ideal, but it is unrealistic.

6. REPORTS AND RECORDS

Since reports and records are necessary for schools to operate efficiently, you must find the most effective and easiest plan to complete them. Energy that could be used on *accomplishing* this task can be expended through *complaints,* if not careful.

The reports and records include monthly reports, commutative records, and report cards. Collect the necessary data in plenty of time (not the day they are due) and get the job behind you.

These reports and records need to be completed correctly and neatly. They become permanent records that will be used throughout a child's life. Do your best.

All of the non-teaching essentials are a part of the teacher's job. They require hours of extra time. Accept them and do them with thanksgiving (Ephesians 5:20). You will be aware of the difference in your attitude toward your job.

Teaching is more than giving out information and mimeographed papers. It also includes being ready and willing to help your students grow and mature into the individuals God wants them to be. It includes supervision outside the classroom and being interested in the child's physical development, his activities, his home, and most importantly, his spiritual welfare and development.

Your reputation as an effective joyful laborer when dealing with these details may make the difference between your being considered a good teacher or your being known as a great one!

Chapter Five

Discipline Suggestions

There are various techniques used by teachers to keep proper control of their classes. Each teacher is an individual, therefore, techniques that work for one may need to be altered for another. Each person also has different toleration levels. One teacher may permit quiet talking during certain periods of the day, but another teacher may not. However, most teachers will agree that students must pay attention when instruction is being given and that disobedience or defiance should not be tolerated.

The scriptures give specific guidelines about disciplining children. Proverbs 13:24 states: "He who spares his rod hates his son, but he who loves him disciplines him diligently." Proverbs 29:17 promises that if you "correct your son, he will give you comfort; he will also delight your soul." God made us and He knows that we need discipline. A Christian school is an extension of the home, and a teacher has the responsibility to discipline students in the classroom. There is definitely a scriptural basis for discipline.

The following guidelines may prove helpful as you strive toward a classroom of self-disciplined students.

1. SEE THIRTY AT A TIME

If you look straight ahead, you can use your peripheral vision. You must be aware of the whole class and not just a few students. A teacher can even position himself so that he can see the whole class while writing on the board instead of "losing" himself at the board.

2. BE AWARE OF YOUR LIMITS

When you feel as if you are losing control, do something at that moment. Do not wait until the class is in chaos. You might turn to the board and write, "Anyone found out of his seat when I finish writing this will lose ten minutes of free time." If everyone is not seated in the allotted time, you MUST follow through with those who did not do as you asked. In a calm voice you can then review rules for proper behavior or continue with classwork. If you do not have recess duty, the disturbers may sit by the building or position themselves by the person on duty so that they can be supervised. Some teachers may require the students to remain at their desks until a timer buzzes or lose free time given to other students in the classroom.

The teacher cannot leave the students alone in the classroom. He must supervise any student that remains in the room and may leave only when all students have been dismissed. You are responsible for the students while they are under your supervision.

3. DETECT PATTERNS OF BEHAVIOR

Certain students tend to create the majority of the disturbances. Locate these as soon as possible and arrange the seating to accommodate them. Perhaps surrounding them with quiet students or placing them at a distance from all their friends will help. Attempt to understand the reasons behind their misbehavior, and then you can make an effort to treat the problem instead of just the symptoms. If they seem to need your special attention, make a practice of patting them on the back when you walk past their desk, or make positive comments to them at any time you see them, such as, "It is so good to see you today," or "Thanks for writing so neatly," or "I like your shirt." If they seem to have extra time, give them an extra project or enrichment assignment. If they jump up often, whisper praise in their ear when they remain in their seats for just five minutes.

4. BE POSITIVE AND EXPECT GOOD BEHAVIOR

On the first day of class tell them, "I expect you to act like the excellent group you are. I know you want to be all that God wants you to be." Proceed to go over the rules for good behavior and emphasize to them that you are the authority in place of their parents, and that God has told us in His word that parents are to discipline their children, and that you as the teacher stand in for the parents while the children are in school.

You need to go over your discipline plan with them. (You must have a plan!) You might have a corner of the board where names are placed for good behavior. The list of names could be written under a smiling face. Their reward could be that they get to go out five minutes early, that they get at the head of the line, that they get to choose their partner for the field trip, that they earn a good behavior note to take home, or any other small recognition strategy. Students will respond to recognition and praise, and it is more pleasant for everyone for you to have this emphasis in the discipline plan you intend to use. If you have never tried it, try it soon—it works! Many teachers who emphasize the positive have excellent control. The students who are responding correctly have to be recognized each class period, so it does require effort and retraining if you are not accustomed to being positive and joyful always!

If it is necessary to place students' names on the opposite corner of the board (and it probably will be necessary), then the first penalty could be a warning, and the penalty on the second offense could be that they write down what they were doing and what they should have been doing. The length of the assignments should vary according to the age of the student. Scripture that deals with the problem could be copied and/or memorized. Further offenses could necessitate calling the parents, isolating the student from the group, sending him to the principal, or if necessary, spanking, if approved.

5. UTILIZE SIGNALS

Signals can tell the class that everyone needs to be quiet without the teacher having to scream over them. One technique is to begin counting. (Any time after 3 that is counted while the class quietens down is free time taken away.) Other ideas include turning the light switch on and off, ringing a bell, or standing facing the class without smiling or saying anything.

Your objective should be to help all the students in your class to become self-disciplined. Through you, Christ can love even the most unlovely child. I John 4:7, 8: "Beloved, let us love one another, for love is from God; and everyone who loves is born of God and knows God. The one who does not love does not know God, for God is love."

If your discipline is done through the eyes of love and you seek to love as Christ loves, then your efforts will be blessed. I John 4:12 states: "If we love one another, God abides in us, and His love is perfected in us."

Chapter Six

Room Appearance

A first impression is made when an administrator, another teacher, parents, or students step into your classroom. Consciously or unconsciously they decide whether you are organized, unorganized, neat, or untidy. This impression causes them to make conclusions about your teaching. Perhaps that seems unfair, but at least it is something over which you can have control. Any teacher can have a neat, orderly, bright room if he is willing to expend the energy. I Corinthians 14:40 tells us to "let all things be done decently and in order."

1. ROOM ARRANGEMENT

First of all, take a sweeping glance around the room and decide if the students' desks, your desk, and any additional furniture are in the best positions for the purpose of teaching. Generally, it is best for the students' desks to face the chalk board with the smallest possible number of desks in each row. In other words, make as many rows as possible so that each row will have fewer students in the back of the room. Put away all materials that need to be stored and have only those materials out that will be used. If possible, provide room for a "center." That can be a table or space for extra projects or for reading. If there are curtains or blinds on the windows, attempt to keep them neat, clean, and straight.

2. ORGANIZE

Provide racks, boxes, or spaces for papers that will be received or returned. This may save you hours of sorting and shuffling through papers if both the students and you know how papers are organized.

Try to keep stacks of materials and papers out of sight so that the room does not become cluttered and confusing. Organize so that everything has a place.

3. BULLETIN BOARDS

Classroom bulletin boards vary greatly in number and size. Some rooms have boards on three walls while some may not have any. If your room has none, then find out what material is safe to use on the wall and tape off spaces to use. Bulletin boards can readily add to the atmosphere of a room.

The letters used can be commercial, cut from squares by the teacher, or formed by using straws, cotton balls, rope, or lettered-on strips to staple to the board. The background can be of such material as paper, fabric, newspaper, wallpaper, aluminum foil, or wrapping paper. The board borders can be trimmed with corrugated pre-cut trim, rick-rack, strips, or lace. Consider the possibilities of color that can be used and begin designing. Keep in mind several principles as you create. These include: Keep the design simple, do not clutter the board, and keep the emphasis of the board away from the edge of the corners—it should be in a prominent place.

There are several types of bulletin-board designs. One is the season board that is changed every month. Another type emphasizes the academics or subject areas that you teach. A third type is the board that includes students' work.

Ideas for bulletin boards for each month are given on the following pages. These may be enlarged by using the opaque projector. Simply project the image to be traced onto a piece of paper taped to the wall or board and trace as large as desired by adjusting the distance between the machine and the paper. An overhead projector also may be used by tracing the picture onto a transparency. The students can help you by coloring the images you trace. Be careful not to have a cluttered room. Too much on the walls and hanging from the ceiling may confuse the learners instead of aiding them.

Anyone can have a bright and cheerful atmosphere in his classroom if he is willing to put forth the effort. As a Christian teacher remember that, "Whatsoever thy hand findeth to do, do it with thy might" (Ecclesiastes 9:10).

The bulletin board ideas on the following pages may be altered for any level and are appropriate for the Christian classroom. Some examples for each idea are given in the appendix.

---

1. September

Directions:

Give each child one-half piece of construction paper. Use fall colors and let each one cut out a leaf after you have discussed the different types of leaves and their shapes. The children put their names on the leaf and then they may be added to the bulletin board to complete the tree. A suggested verse to put on the board is John 15:5, "I am the vine, ye are the branches: He that abideth in me, and I in him, the same bringeth forth much fruit: for 'Without me ye can do nothing.' "

2. October

Directions:

Each child cuts an orange pumpkin from orange paper. Light and dark pumpkin leaves may be added along two edges of the board. The children's papers are stapled to the pumpkins. These can include a Bible lesson illustrated, a creative paper, information gathered about pumpkins, or any academic or art paper selected for the board.

Variations:

Pumpkin leaves can be used as backing for student work. They may be attached to vines running from the pumpkin examples.

3. November

Directions:

Papers can be added to the board that:

1. list things for which they are thankful
2. tell how they will spend Thanksgiving
3. depict the first Thanksgiving
4. summarize information they have researched about the first Thanksgiving
5. list scriptures about being thankful

Variations:

Fall pictures may be posted around the Pilgrims, or pictures of the students and/or their families.

4. December

Directions:

Use Christmas cards (Christian ones when possible) to make the shape of a tree. Use ornaments and/or ribbons to decorate it. The children may help by bringing in old cards from home.

Variations:

Students may make their own Christmas cards to be posted. These may be made by:

1. using stencils and trace or spatter paint
2. cutting and pasting pictures
3. creating their own design or picture
4. using scraps of wrapping paper, ribbon, etc. to create a design

5. January

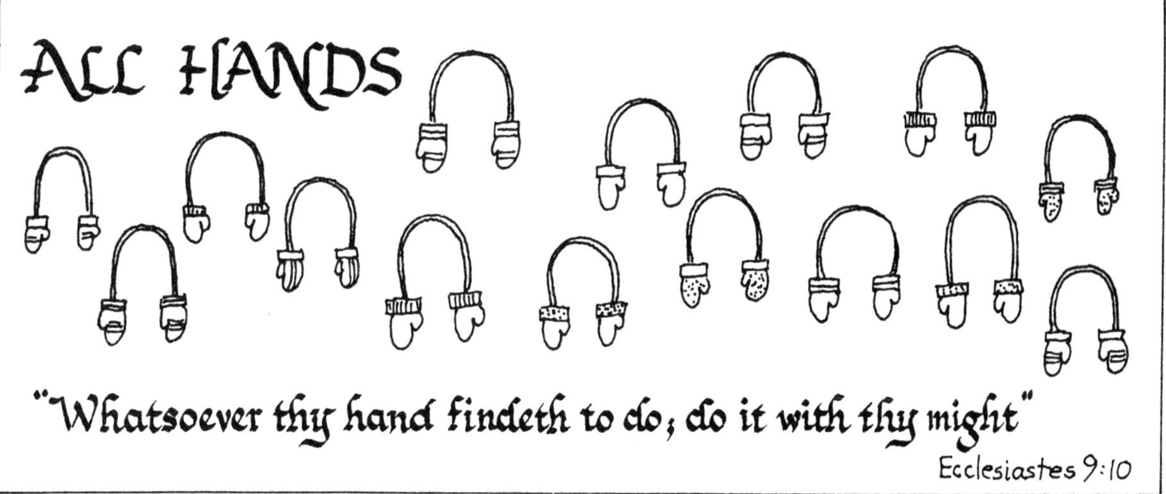

Directions:

The children cut out a mitten or their hand shape and put their name on it. A piece of yarn is used to connect them.

Variation:

The students may cut out two glove patterns for each hand, staple them together around the edges and stuff with newspaper.

5. January (alternate)

Directions:

The older students may draw and color a picture in the shape of a square. They may illustrate a winter scene or any academic subject being studied. Paste trim around the square for a patch. Rick-rack, lace, or paper may be used. Attached these to the board so that it looks like a patch-work winter quilt.

6. February

Directions:

Decorate a large heart and place a verse about love in the center. Use the silhouettes of Washington and Lincoln and place information about these two presidents underneath their pictures.

Variations:

Older students may research these two presidents. Either decide as a class the facts to post or post two of the best reports. Students could also enter a contest to find the best verse about the "heart."

7. March

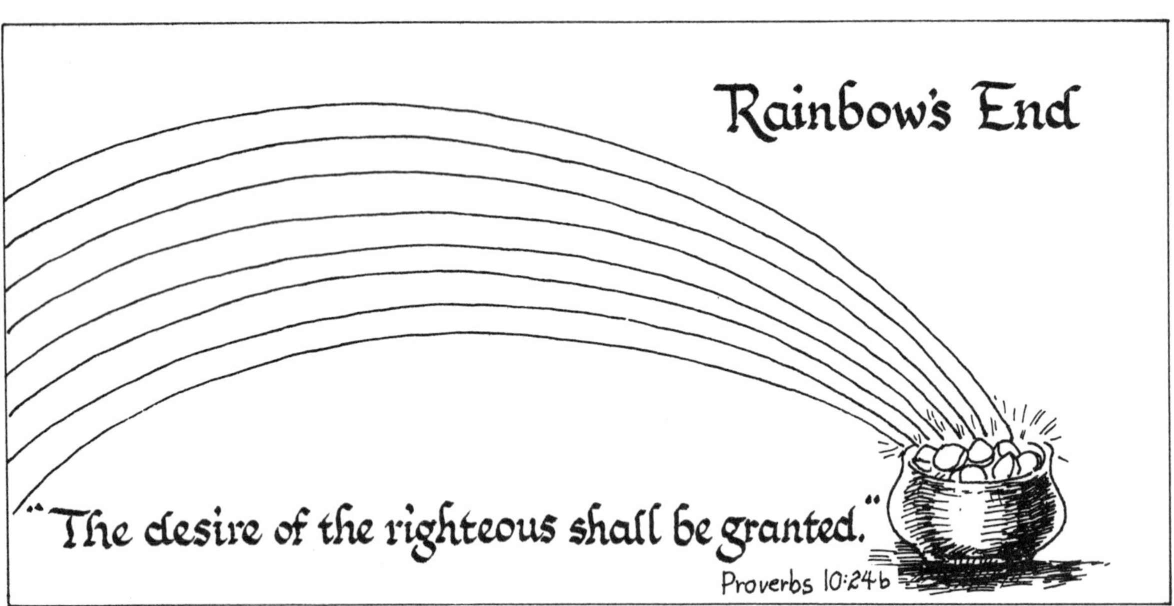

Directions:

Make a colorful rainbow using crepe paper strips. Gold wrapping paper can be used for the pot of gold. Let each student cut a gold piece and write on them what they would like to...

1. accomplish the remainder of the year (academically and spiritually)
2. do when they grow up
3. do this month
4. do during spring vacation
5. have right now

8. April

Directions:

The students may submit titles and scripture references to be used on the board. You could also give them an opportunity to hand in a design for the Easter board.

Directions:

Flower blooms are used for each square of the calendar. They are displayed over the board during the month. Students' papers displayed can be changed throughout the month.

9. May

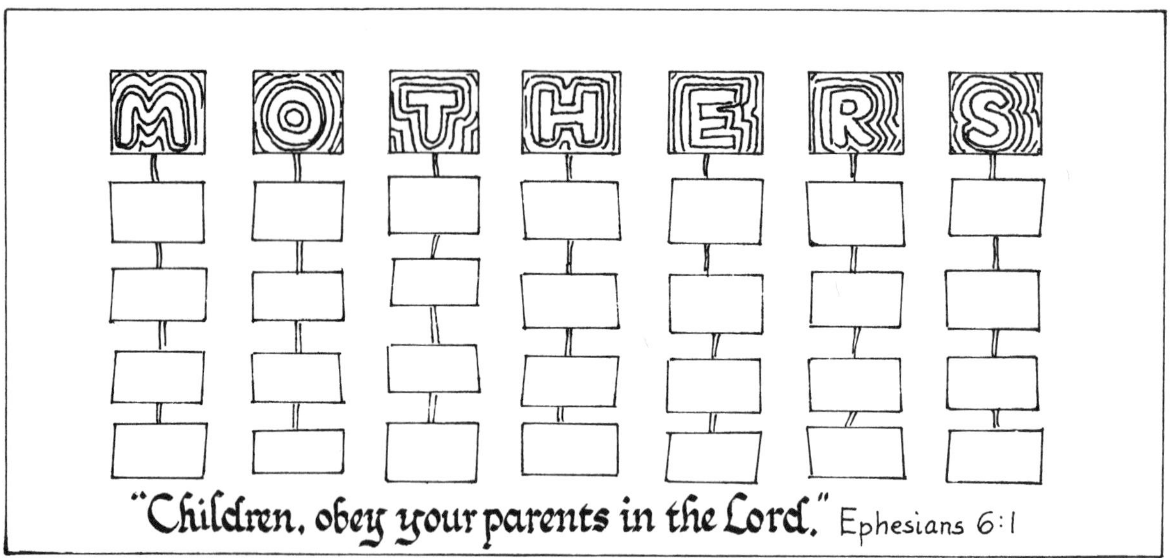

Directions and Variations:

Each child may do the following to be displayed:

1. write a verse or prose to their mother
2. draw a picture of their mother's face
3. write a description of their mother

Yarn or ribbon is used to connect the papers. Large jar lid rims may be used to frame the pictures if they are cut in a round shape.

10. June

Directions:

Either "son" or "sun" may be used. Each student signs his name and may include some information about their summer. Differently colored magic markers or black may be used for each signature.

Variations:

The students may write what they plan to do during the summer and display their plans on the board.

Chapter Seven

Motivating Students

You have probably heard the adage, "You can lead a horse to water, but you can't make him drink." That may be true, but you can make him thirsty. Then he will want to drink. This chapter gives some strategies for making students thirst for knowledge. Of course, we as Christians know the source of the living water and need to keep in mind that the students who receive this life-changing message have life's greatest motivation. Jesus said to the woman at the well, "But whosoever drinketh of the water that I shall give him shall never thirst; but the water that I shall give him shall be in him a well of water springing up into everlasting life" (John 4:14).

You will find the following list helpful as you consider motivating each student to his God-given capacity in the area of academics.

1. INTERESTS

Study the child carefully to discern his interests, natural abilities, and his unusual knowledge or experiences. Involve him in activities that require the use of these talents. Allow him to be successful and he will appear in a favorable light to his peers. If he is not popular, he will need this positive experience. Have an accepting atmosphere in your class and do not allow the children to criticize others. This bad habit seems to be naturally acquired, and to overcome it requires determination, disipline, maturity, and the Holy Spirit working in our lives. Seeing the faults of others and excusing our own is dealt with in Matthew 7:1-5. We are told that the way we treat others is the way we will be treated, and that while we are trying to point out something negative about another person, it is small and insignificant compared to our own "beam." Also, continually remind the children of the golden rule. It works whenever and wherever people need to work cooperatively together! (Luke 6:31)

An accepting atmosphere in your classroom allows students to express their opinions more freely and to not be afraid to fail. Their interests and experiences can be used positively and successfully. . .if you are aware of them and if you provide an accepting atmosphere.

2. REWARDS

In some cases, students will work to please their teacher and his approval provides the motivation needed. Many children complete tasks to gain favor in the teacher's eyes. You are a significant person in their lives.

For others, grades are the incentive. A child's need to make good grades may come from within. He may possess a natural curiosity. He studies and reads for the joy of learning. Do not expect too many of these! However, at certain levels and for certain subject areas many will demonstrate this natural curiosity. That's the reason you need to think through a motivational activity for lessons you teach. Arouse their curiosity before giving instructions.

Some students are motivated by external forces or extrinsic rewards. Anything from pieces of candy or peanuts to extra P.E. or recess time may be utilized. Other suggestions for rewards are stickers, parties, stars, or certain privileges such as getting to go to lunch first or going on a picnic with the teacher for lunch.

Generally, children are motivated to complete a task if they realize that they are the ones benefiting from the activity. Some are mature enough to work toward long-term goals, such as their future jobs, and realize that their future career is at stake. They desire to do well. For others, very short-term goals work best—such as raisins or nuts for a neat, completed assignment. Students want to know, "How does this benefit me?"

3. PRAISE

Being praised is enough reward for some. Everyone enjoys receiving a "well done," especially from peers or employers. Children have the same feeling. You, as the teacher, can teach the students to praise each other in tasks accomplished well, skills mastered, or talents shared with the class. Show by example how to praise and let it be a natural outflow of your personality. Be sincere but liberal with your praise and it will be returned to you. Luke 6:38 states, "Give, and it shall be given unto you; good measure, pressed down, and shaken together, and running over, shall men give unto your bosom. For with the same measure that ye mete withal it shall be measured to you again." You are the model before them. Praise, rather than tearing down personalities with sarcasm. You may write notes or messages to the student, and he will have something to show to his parents, as well as a reminder of the contented, satisfied feeling that praise can bring. Some children may not work for praise alone, but because their self-esteem is increased by praise, they will be able to put more energy into their studies. Praise is free. It can be given easily. It does much good. Try it. You'll like it, and your students will too!

Your responsibility as the teacher will be to use the motivational strategies that work best for your students. Also, try techniques that you observe others using, or modify them to fit your group. Remember that children who are highly motivated and challenged learn faster and are a joy to teach.

Volumes have been written about motivation, but there is still no single "best" technique to use for all students. A combination of the ideas discussed in this chapter is normally utilized. The teacher's goal is to help the child become self-motivated. Hopefully, he will desire to be the best that he can be in every area of his life. His aims and goals should not necessarily depend upon his circumstances or surroundings. If he is motivated from within, he can become all that God intended him to be. Keep your students reminded of Paul's words in Philippians 4:13: "I can do ALL things through Christ which strengtheneth me."

Chapter Eight

Diagnosing Student Needs

Teachers should evaluate students to determine their level of competence and then should teach them on that level. You need to test the students in order to diagnose their strengths and weaknesses and take them from the known to the unknown. You do not teach them on the level where you wish they were, or where they ought to be, but where they are actually performing. You may have to teach above the level where you are assigned, or below it. Usually, as the grade level increases, so does the spread of abilities in the class. For this reason, you will probably be utilizing grouping in your classroom for some subjects and will be teaching on various levels.

This chapter suggests ways to diagnose students so that you may plan to meet their academic needs.

1. TEACHER OBSERVATION AND PLANNING

You will probably be diagnosing the students' knowledge every day as you observe their daily assignments. This information enables you to determine whether you need to spend more time on long division, or a certain sound in phonics, or to forge ahead to another new and different concept.

A teacher's keen observation can give a legitimate evaluation of a child's ability. Train yourself to watch for patterns in the students' work. Do they seem to be subtracting incorrectly every time on their division problems, or do they not know the multiplication tables? Usually you will find that you cannot wait until everyone has mastered every skill before you move on to another lesson. However, there are certain basic concepts that should be learned at each grade level. Try all resources available (parents, peer teachers, group work, etc.) to ensure mastery by each student. Sometimes a student is not mature enough or has a learning disability that will impede his progression at a normal rate. You may be frustrating yourself and the student if you are not careful to remember individual differences in capabilities.

What can you do to keep the brighter students on task while some of the others are grasping for understanding? Some ideas to use with them are listed below.

a. Library books

Let the students visit the school library every two or three weeks and have them keep their library book at their desk. When they complete their book, let them record it on a form you provide, or make a booklet for the library table. Let them make a poster to illustrate the book or add links to a bookworm that shows the book, author, and reader. Certificates or rewards may be given for books read.

b. Write

Have them write a reader's theatre, a play, or choral reading for the class to perform.

c. Class newspaper

Students may write a class newspaper and be in charge of getting it prepared for you to make copies for the class.

d. Enrichment activities

Plan some enrichment activities (not more of the same kinds of problems or assignments, but deeper into the subject) and place directions on cards or in folders to be placed in a certain area of the room. Students may choose one to complete. Also, individual folders can be prepared. If the class is studying about 300 animals, let them choose one to research and then display their work or give them an opportunity to share with the class.

e. Responsibility

Give them the responsibility to plan a chapel devotional and have them prepare visual aids for it.

f. Tutor

Assign them to another student(s) to be a peer tutor. You do not want to overdo this one, but they can also learn from the experience.

These students can work independently and the teacher is then free to help those students who need his attention.

2. PAST RECORDS

Most of the time a student's past record is available to you in the form of a cumulative folder. The "cum" folders contain the student's grades and achievement scores. Each year's results are added to this record. Sometimes they may also contain teacher comments. You should not let a previous comment influence you for or against a student before you even get to know him. However, if he has been in school for several years, you may see a pattern of behavior that may be useful. Sometimes students react differently for another teacher. Just be certain that you do not pronounce an individual "guilty" unless he proves it to you. If you are required to write comments after you have taught the students, remember to keep them as professional as possible and attempt to refrain from negativism or biased statements.

The achievement scores that are recorded each year will be from standardized tests that have been used to test large numbers of students. The Stanford Achievement Test (SAT) is an example. A grade-equivalent score of 5.4 would mean that the student scored fifth grade and fourth month. If he is in the fifth grade and the test is given in May, he should score 5.8 to be exactly where he should be at that time.

If a stanine score is given, it will be a number between one and nine (Standard nine). The scores from the test are divided into nine parts. A score of 5 indicates average ability, a score of one indicates very low ability; and a score of 9 is indicative of high ability. A percentile score might also be shown. This score indicates how a student compares with all the other students tested and indicates the percent of the individuals in that group whom he surpasses.

3. INFORMAL TESTING

"Informal" tests are ones that are not standardized. They may be published or can be compiled by a teacher. There are several tests for reading that are published and which would be considered "informal."

1. *The San Diego State Quick Assessment* was prepared by Margaret LaPray and Ramon Ross of San Diego State University. It was printed in the *Journal of Reading,* January 1969. It is a quick way to determine a student's reading ability by presenting to him letters and words from certain reading levels. It can be given in a few minutes. (The more advanced the student, the longer it will take to complete.)

2. *Sucher-Allred Reading Placement Inventory* (mentioned in Chapter 1) is by Floyd Sucher and Ruel Allred of Brigham Young University and is published by The Economy Company. The teacher's manual contains information for identifying a student's independent, instructional, and frustrational reading levels, and also for identifying common word-recognition and comprehension errors. Student booklets are also available. It can be given in about twenty minutes.

Margaret LaPray has also published a book of informal reading tests, *On the Spot Reading Diagnosis File,* published by The Center for Applied Research in Education, Inc., in West Nyack, New York 10994. There are seven areas in reading assessment given in the book: visual, auditory and motor development, readiness, letter and word skills, skills with phrases, sentence skills, paragraph skills, and affective measures.

3. PUBLISHED TESTS

The Woodcock Reading Mastery Test has been discussed in Chapter 1. It tests students K-12 and can be administered and scored in thirty-four minutes. Another test published by the American Guidance Service, Inc. (Circle Pines, Minnesota 55014) is the Peabody Individual Achievement Test. It provides a wide-range screening measure of achievement in the areas of mathematics, reading, spelling, and general information for grades K-adult. It can be administered and scored in thirty to forty minutes. You probably will not be able to test all of your students on this individual test because of the time involved. However, the children about whom you need more information can be diagnosed explicity by this test.

The Wide Range Achievement Test (WRAT) may be considered for measuring a student's performance level in reading, spelling, and math. Disabilities should be revealed in any of those areas. There are two levels of the test, Level I (5 years-11 years) and Level II (12-adulthood). It can be administered and scored in twenty to thirty minutes. The test was written by Joseph and Sarah Jastak and is published by Guidance Associates of Delaware, Inc., 1526 Gilpin Avenue, Wilmington, Delaware 19806.

Intelligence is an important variable in learning. However, it is not everything. If you think a student's problem may be his low I.Q., you may test your entire class with the Otis Quick Scoring I.Q. Test to be sure. You may also use an individual Intelligence Test such as the Slosson Intelligence Test (SIT) which is published by Slosson Educational Publications, Inc., P. O. Box 280, East Aurora, New York 14052. Test completion time varies from 10 to 15 minutes for the average person. The test measures pre-school children through adults and is easy to administer and score. Usually, students with I.Q.s over 130 are considered for gifted programs; those with I.Q.s from 90-109 are considered average; and those with I.Q.s under 90 are considered for slow-learner classes.

God uses tests in our daily lives to help us grow. Job was tested, obeyed God, and was given twice as much as he had before. David, Moses, and Peter were also tested and their failures and weaknesses were recorded in the scriptures so that we can know how God can forgive and continue to use our lives—even when we fail. Also God gave us a promise about testing and temptation: "There hath no temptation [testing] taken you but such as is common to man: but God is faithful, who will not suffer you to be tempted [tested] above that ye are able; but will with the temptation also make a way to escape, that ye may be able to bear it" (I Corinthians 10:13). When we are tested, we need to claim the foregoing promise and escape through the way He has provided. We cannot stay in the situation many times and cope with it. Our responsibility is to get out through the provision He offers and to teach our students to do the same. Sometimes solving life's problems can be difficult, but life is made up of problem-solving. Isn't it exciting to know that we have a way of escape and that we serve the one who has given us true answers to life's dilemmas?

Chapter Nine

Teaching Slow Learners

Most self-contained, heterogeneous classrooms will contain slow learners. They can learn, but at a slower rate than the others in the class. Dealing with them requires patience and understanding. James 5:11 says, "Behold we count those blessed who endured. You have heard of the patience of Job, and have seen the outcome of the Lord's dealings, that the Lord is full of compassion and is merciful." You must develop and exercise patience to be successful with this group.

In order to reach the slow learners, the teacher needs to teach the student, not the book. There is no proven method to make students learn. You have to motivate the student and get him excited about learning. The method is never the same with any two students. The most successful method is any way that you feel works with a particular child. The materials you use are not as important as making the child see himself as a loved, appreciated person created in God's image. He made us "just lower than the angels and crowned us with glory and honor" (Psalms 8).

1. PRAISE

Simply saying "good" for a correct answer or for some evident improvement is positive, but is not as effective as praise. Give praise and more praise! This may be done by telling the group, "Boy, did Jamie do well today!" You may want to let him show the teacher he had last year what he can do, or let him demonstrate, teach, or read something to a younger group. He then has been recognized, has been successful, and is excited about the next step he is going to take. *Assure success by keeping each step of learning within a child's grasp.* There seems to be a direct correlation between the amount of praise given and learning.

Think of yourself as waving a fan and trying desperately to keep a small spark from going out. This is an example of the teacher trying to excite the slow student about learning. You have to attempt to ignite that small spark and get it flaming.

Explain to the group that practicing their skills is similar to playing soccer, basketball, baseball, or the piano. The more they practice, the better they will become.

If you are working with the slow learners in reading, let them repeat a sentence until they can read it well. See which one can read it the best, or ask for a certain word and see who can find it on the page first. In math, put up the same problem on both sides of the board. Let two students in the class work on the board and race to see who can solve the problem first. For language, use children's names in the sentences and phrases being studied, or let the students illustrate vocabulary words that will be used in a mural or bulletin board.

Plan ways to use your God-given creativity more effectively. Keep in mind that children need to be successful at the tasks assigned, and that published material or mimeographed sheets do not have to be used exclusively. Plan more activities than you think you will need, and then you will always have ideas ready.

2. PARENTS

Most parents are very interested in their child's progress. If they realize that he is behind the group in academics, you probably can enlist them to give assistance.

One effective idea in reading is to ask the parents to let their child read to them at least fifteen minutes a day. Sometimes an older sibling can help. The results can be phenomenal! Some children have increased their time to thirty minutes and have included the weekend. They found reading to be enjoyable for the first time in their lives. If the reading material is on their level and the parents encourage them, perhaps they will not fight reading anymore.

The teacher will need to supply incentives at school for the home-reading program. You may keep a chart in the room and mark a space for each day the child reads. The child may use a stamp; you may use stickers, or you may want to write in the person's name to whom the child reads. At the end of the month or grading period, a certificate could be sent to that person. You may want to provide a grab bag at school from which the student may choose a gift when he completes a certain number of hours of reading.

Math facts can be practiced at home. Timed skills tests can be given each week at school and the parents informed that the student has passed. At certain levels, a reward can be planned.

3. PARTNERS

The students are divided into pairs. They can work together in whatever subject matter you choose.

In reading, they can take turns reading aloud to each other. Since there will be at least 15 voices at once, you will have to be convinced that all learning does not take place in silence.

The slow learner, for whatever reasons, is a child who is experiencing an uphill struggle in his academic work. When he visualizes the distance he has to go, he gets discouraged even trying. The teacher must take him as far this year as he is willing and able to go.

Remember to give him small assignments and encourage him all the way to completion. Tell him that you can see progress, and let him know that you are there to help. One teacher whispered the correct spelling in one child's ear as she gave out words to the group. Because he could make 100% in spelling that day, his math scores improved also!

If the child is having difficulty in reading, by whatever means available to you, teach him how! Realize that in our world today, everyone needs to know how to read, and that it is your God-given professional responsibility and obligation to teach him how to read. If he is going to special teacher(s), work with them to assure continuity in his program.

When working with the slow learner, realize that he *can* learn—just at a slower rate. Demand that slow learners work as hard for you as you work with them. Double your efforts and reach out in love. Great will be your reward!

Chapter Ten

Parent-Teacher Conferences

Parent-Teacher conferences may be a regular program at your school. A note is written to the parents at a specific time each year, and they all sign up for a 15-20 minute individual conference with the teacher. Usually the teacher writes an available time on the note, the parent signs the slip, and the child brings it back to school. The students are usually dismissed for half a day for two or three days to give the teacher release time for the conferences. Normally, the child concerned is not present during the parent-teacher conference.

Administrators usually permit the teacher or the parent to schedule an individual conference when needed. A time may be set after or before school hours for parent(s) to meet with the teacher. Parents should be aware of the fact that they cannot go directly to your room. They should go to the office and should be advised as to when and where they may talk with the teacher. Irate parents could disturb the entire class if they were permitted to barge directly into the classroom. Class time need not be interrupted for conferences.

Parent-teacher conferences can be a most positive experience or the most dreaded encounter of the year. Success depends upon your ability to communicate with other people and your readiness to share ideas, information, burdens, hurts, and frustrations. The following will aid you in making a conference easier and more beneficial for everyone involved, especially for the student.

1. REALIZE THAT YOU SPEAK WITH EXPERTS

Teachers sometimes feel that since they are with the student seven or eight hours a day for five days a week, they know a child better than anyone else; but parents know their child as well or better than you do. Granted, you may see him differently than his Mom or Dad sees him, but they had him for at least six years before you met him. They also have him during weekends, summers, and vacations. They look at him through eyes of love, and that covers a lot of mistakes and problems. (I Peter 4:8b, "For love shall cover the multitude of sins.") They know their child well but may view his shortcomings differently than you do. They see him isolated, but you see him in a society of peers, while he is struggling for a position among them.

2. USE "SOME" AND "SEEM" A LOT

In other words, don't be dogmatic. Leave yourself a loophole. For example, say, "It *seems* that Joey sometimes does not hand in his homework," or "He *seems* not to be listening in class." Instead of "He interrupts the class constantly," say "*Some* days I have to correct him." Stay away from "He *never* does his homework," or "He *always* talks too much." Soften your language to keep from putting the parent on the defensive. ("A soft answer turneth away wrath: but grievous words stir up anger." Proverbs 15:1)

3. HAVE PROOF

Have samples available of the student's work. Have handwriting or special projects in order to show the parent his child's progress. Poor papers may have a way of getting lost or forgotten and may not get into the parent's hand. If the proof is there, then what you think is not pitted against what the child or parent thinks. You can truthfully say how the child is doing and will be able to back up what you say. Having some samples of his work, not just a few grades for class discussion and participation, goes a long way in helping you make your point.

4. KNOW THE CHILD, NOT JUST HIS GRADE

Teachers tend to get so busy with the students' papers—grading and averaging tests—that they forget how much parents appreciate the teacher getting to know their child. Be able to tell his parents something you have noticed about his caring for others, about being friendly, about being a leader, or about being interested in sports, music, or class games. Take time to understand the child's cares, fears, or desires, and share this understanding with the persons who have more interest in this child than you do. Parents feel that you really care about their offspring if you are interested enough to take this extra step of involvement. A good anecdotal story helps to illustrate your observation.

5. PROVIDE A PRESCRIPTION

Doctors know that if they give their patients something to do, or take, they feel better about the illness and the physician. Soaking in water daily, drinking more fluids, or gargling with salt water gives the patients the idea that things are going to get better faster. As teachers, we sometimes need to apply the same reasoning. If children have problems, parents want to *do something* to help their offspring. Therefore, before any conference with parents, make sure that you list—either mentally or literally—some things that parents can do to help the situation. The solution might be to let their child read to them for ten minutes at night, or to provide an hour of unscheduled quiet time for homework every night without television, radio, or phone calls. Perhaps bi-weekly conferences should be scheduled for a period of time so that parents can keep closer check on daily assignments and weekly tests. Have a short prescription ready for a parent whose child is having problems in school, and the parent will love you for it.

6. WATCH THE HEDGES

If the child is having a problem in your class, advise the parent. Don't "beat around the bush" and have the parent confused as to why his child is stumbling or failing. You can be frank without being rude or cruel. You can be honest without being hateful or vindictive. Be kind but truthful. (Proverbs 31:26 states that "She openeth her mouth with wisdom; and in her tongue is the law of kindness.")

If the child is having trouble with fifth grade social studies, and you know he is reading on a second grade level, make that clear to the parent. Tell the parent, "We must work together to bring his reading level up before he gets lost in volumes of undigested material." Do not be vague. Do not be afraid to discuss the problem. If you or the parent have requested an individual conference, most likely there is a problem present that should be discussed.

7. BE AN EXPERT WITH CAUTION

You should know the subject matter you are to teach and have objectives for your instruction. Be careful about coming across to parents as a "know-it-all," because some parents will set out to prove that you do *not* know it all. Stand your ground when you know you are right, but be careful about being inflexible and about being perfect in all your judgments. Be aware of the many ways to accomplish goals, and be willing to try an alternative solution. You may have to confess that you need assistance or that you would be willing to try another plan. ("For the Lord giveth wisdom: out of His mouth cometh knowledge and understanding." Proverbs 2:6)

8. SLAY THE DRAGONS

It would be unfair to leave you with the impression that all parents will be nice to you if you are nice to them, or that both parents will rush down in enthusiastic anticipation of a parent-teacher conference. In the real world, sometimes you meet parents who are dragons. They breathe fire upon your head, and you would not dare send home anything that had not been double-checked twice. These dragons whip their tail of authority around and would tell you, the principal, and the school board how to run the system. The best advice is to listen and to have the principal with you for the conference, especially if he backs you (as most will do). Speak softly and without anger, but have your strategies thought through (Proverbs 15:1). Know where you stand and stand firmly. Always remember to keep your student's best interest at the heart of the matter. Dragon conferences can be unnerving, belittling, and unsettling. Just keep in mind that there are not many dragons around.

9. KEEP YOUR VISION

Never let the conference time cloud the image of your class members. Meeting parents can be an asset. You will understand the child better. Face the reality of the child's world, and realize that he tells things as *he* sees them, rather than as they appear to an adult. One father, as he sat down with his child's first-grade teacher, chuckled, "You believe half of what Susie tells you about our home, and we'll believe half of what she tells us about school."

Teachers tend to feel that parents do not care about their child's growth or progress if they do not attend the conference. Sometimes they are afraid to come. At other times they feel that the news will be negative, as it has been in previous conferences. They may think that they are doing all they can do and that little else can be done. If the child's parents happen to be dragons and intimidate you, be careful not to take out your frustrations on the child. He cannot change his parents. He did not choose them. He may be embarrassed by their behavior.

Keep clear in your mind that you are working with impressionable individuals. Your objective should be to mold these lives that have been entrusted to your care to the very best of your ability. Jesus certainly stressed the children's importance when the disciples tried to brush them aside, but the Master Designer of us all, as well as the universe, called the children to Himself and said, "Suffer little children, and forbid them not to come unto me: for of such is the kingdom of heaven" (Matthew 19:14). On another occasion Jesus used a child to teach the disciples about who would be the greatest in heaven. "Jesus called a little child unto Him, and set him in the midst of them. And said, verily I say unto you, except ye be converted and become as little children, ye shall not enter into the kingdom of heaven" (Matthew 18:2, 3).

Parents are wonderful in most cases. They can become your friends for life, as well as help you to teach more effectively. Parents' active involvement in their child's school is most important if the school is to reach excellence in education.

Chapter Eleven

Interpersonal Relationships

"As a man thinketh in his heart so is he" (Proverbs 23:7). How do you work with others? How do you view your work? Teachers quickly earn a reputation of either being cooperative with a quiet and gentle spirit (II Timothy 2:24) or being a criticizer and a complainer. If your thoughts are as they should be, then so will be your actions. One thing is for certain: your attitude will be showing!

Your attitude toward your work and others with whom you serve can limit or expand your effectiveness as a teacher. You especially need to be aware of your attitude in regard to the areas listed and discussed below.

1. SCHOOL PERSONNEL

a. Principals

Teachers may be unaware of the principal's many responsibilities. Consider his load, and realize that you are not there to do his job, but you have been called to teach. We are all a necessary part of the body of Christ and have our own individual calling (I Corinthians 12:12). The principal cannot please everyone and neither can you. You need to build up your brother and sister, not tear them down (I John 2:10, I John 4:7, 8).

The principal is an authority over you. Working with him—and not against him—is most important. You might even have to call on him to give you a recommendation for another job in the future (Proverbs 22:1). Most principals will listen and assist you in any way possible if you are doing your job well and if you approach them with a loving spirit. They are more likely to listen and react to your observations and requests if you have them infrequently, rather than every day at 2:30 p.m.

Like husbands in the family, principals in schools make decisions that will affect everyone involved. However, the principal is also responsible for and has to deal with the outcome of them. Your obligation is to support him and pray for him. If a problem arises which you think needs his attention, go to him first, not to your fellow teachers or parents (Matthew 5:24 NASB). Working together cooperatively will accomplish the jobs that each is called to do.

b. Colleagues

Your attitude toward your colleagues can be either helpful or damaging to all and to the work each is striving to accomplish. Keep in mind that as you are loving, kind, responsive, and helpful toward them, you are exemplifying biblical principles (Matthew 7:12 NASB). Hopefully, they will do the same toward you. Remember, you are the student's model, even in the area of dealing with your peers.

Attempt to assist if another teacher needs help with their duties, if a new teacher needs direction, or if you can be cooperative and flexible by allowing a change in your schedule to accommodate a special request from another class (such as seeing a play, hearing their poems or songs, etc.). Your attitude in dealing with other teachers can make a difference between working cooperatively together or pulling against each other.

c. Janitor

One of the most helpful persons to a new teacher can be the janitor or the matinenance personnel (if you are lucky enough to have one). He knows the location of most of the things you will need during the year. Your attitude toward him should be one of kindness and acceptance.

There are ways to show your appreciation for his work and contribution to the school. Save a cupcake for him when the parties are given in your class, or have the class make cards for him at Christmas or on his birthday. Chat with him after school as he sweeps out your room, then you will most likely receive the same attitude and attention as you have shown (Matthew 7:2, Matthew 7:12 NASB).

2. YOUR WORK

Your attitude toward teaching can make a difference in your relationship with your students. If you are not glad you are a teacher, it will be evident to the children and to your peers. As Christians, we are to rejoice always (Philippians 4:4).

How do you face each day? Do you have difficulty being joyful and expectant about your job? Do you live only for weekends? A grumbling, ungrateful heart will certainly show in your face and actions. Repeat Psalm 118:24 each morning and mean it: "This is the day which the Lord hath made, we will rejoice and be glad in it." A joyous nature is contagious, and you will see your students following your example.

3. EXTRAS

Be mentally prepared for extra assignments. At times you may think that no one knows how much a teacher must accomplish. Be assured that every teacher has those same thoughts. Each teacher feels that he is doing as much as possible. If anyone mentions adding another responsibility, teachers tend to respond negatively, no matter how necessary the task may be. You may be asked to serve on a committee, sponsor another group or activity, or be in charge of another program. You may need to make another priority list and place certain tasks on the "back burners" for a time. Try to accept these extra assignments as necessary and vital to a successful total school program. Be positive about these inconveniences. The Lord loves a cheerful giver, and that could include giving of your time and talents as unto Him (II Corinthians 9:6, 7).

4. PARENTS

The parents of the children you teach generally desire the same results as you. This is especially true of those who place their children in a Christian school. They desire to work with you and expect the school to be an extension of the home.

Some of the parents with whom you come in contact may have different ideas and little information about the process of education. Find ways to communicate with them and to work together. Be a great listener and then lovingly explain your procedures and why you are giving certain activities or assignments to their child. Your attitude should show love and respect (I Corinthians 13) rather than exhibit superiority.

Express sincerely that you are interested in their child and are trying to help him. Parents do not like to hear from the teacher that their child is a monster, even though they may realize that he is far from being perfect. Give your professional opinion and sprinkle the discussion with an understanding of the parents' point of view.

Your attitude in dealing with parents can determine whether or not you are successful in obtaining their cooperation. A teacher cannot wear his feelings similar to porcupine quills. Pain may be inflicted unnecessarily, and you, the child, and the school may suffer because you were not effective in dealing with parents.

Attempt to be soothing and turn away their wrath with a soft answer, and have a wholesome tongue (Proverbs 15:1-4). James reminds us about the harm our tongue can inflict—it is like a fire and cannot be tamed. However, if we ask for God's wisdom, then we may demonstrate those Christian qualities of purity, peacefulness, and gentleness. You will be blessed for your efforts (James 3:5-18).

5. CHILDREN

Your attitude toward the children will affect your teaching methods. Do you consider them as individuals with feelings and emotions, or do you simply consider them as images to teach? Are they persons for whom you have concern spiritually, as well as physically and academically? Are they merely steps in your ladder to success, or do you see them as individuals who need your constant concern?

You need to examine your motives. Our Lord considered children so important that he told his disciples to let them come to Him, and He used them as an example of faith (Luke 18:15-17). As teachers, we, too, should consider the children that we have been called to teach as being individuals created in God's image. This attitude will enable you to deal with the students in the spirit of love.

6. FAILURES AND SUCCESSES

There are many trials and errors in teaching. Experience is helpful in determining whether or not an idea will work. However, be encouraged in the fact that other teachers also experience failures. You need not consider yourself an incompetent teacher if you seem to be less than 100 percent effective every week. Learn from your mistakes and step forward.

When you do try an idea or activity that proves successful, then share it with peers, parents, or principal. Others may also like to try it. Give God the glory for working through you. God took almost all of Gideon's army away from him so that *He* would get the glory for the victory, rather than man (Judges 7).

Keep a joyful and thankful heart so that your attitude will be positive. You will find your work more enjoyable and productive, and those with whom you come in contact will also be blessed.

Chapter Twelve

Substituting

As a college-trained professional, there may be a time when you find yourself faced with the job of being a substitute. It may be shortly after you finish college and a teaching job is unavailable, or it may be when your family moves to a new town and there are no openings. You need to be prepared to "sub."

1. ADVANTAGES AND DISADVANTAGES

a. Advantages

Very few teachers choose substituting as a life's vocation, even though there are some advantages to not being the regular teacher:

1. Preparation is minimal.
2. No after-school duties are required.
3. You work only as you choose.
4. You see how districts, schools, and classrooms differ.
5. New procedures and ideas from other teachers are observed.
6. You deal with the problems of a particular class for only one day or a few days.

b. Disadvantages

There are also some disadvantages:

1. The absence of the regular teacher makes it a "sink the sub day" for many students.
2. There are many new names and faces to remember.
3. You never know what day you may be called to teach.
4. There is little continuity in your teaching.
5. You feel that you do not really belong anywhere.

2. YOU AS THE SUBSTITUTE

There are certain things that you can do to prepare for substituting. If you are called early enough in the morning, try to get to school and read through the teacher's plans in order to become acquainted with the schedule. If the students are slated for music, gym, films, art, etc., find out all the necessary information from another teacher or from the secretary. Where do they go for these activities? Do you take them and bring them back or meet them somewhere? Locate the books, teacher's guides, workbooks, or ditto sheets to be used, and make certain you can decipher the code. Many teachers use abbreviations in their planning which might not be familiar to you.

Next, make certain you can find a listing of students for the roll call. The office will have a list if the teacher took the roll book with him. Also, locate a time schedule. You would be surprised how often, whether by ignorance or deceit, the students can give you the incorrect information about when to go to lunch, when to get out for break, or when to go home. "We always go early," is a quote you'll hear quite often. Some students tend to use fictitious names in hopes of making the day less monotonous.

Introduce yourself to some of the other teachers and let them know that you are substituting for the day. They may be unaware that the regular teacher is absent until he fails to show up for lunch! Usually fellow teachers will be supportive and helpful.

Establish yourself from the very beginning as the authority for the day. Explain who you are and inform them about the regular teacher's absence. Normally information is available for you from the absent teacher. It is important to carry out his plans as best you can, even though you may not agree with the assignments or the methods advocated. Your assignment is to see that the job is carried out much like it would be if the teacher were there himself. This is not the place to try out new ideas in education or innovative techniques that you have just learned. If you can fit any of that into the regular plans, then do it.

If the students tell you they always slide in the hall and they always race for the entrance, you can inform them that they will have to wait until their regular teacher comes to do that. While *you* are there, they will line up, walk, and behave as *you* desire.

Remember that you probably will not win any popularity contests with kids while being a substitute. The carnal nature of the students seems to rise to the surface on "sub" day. Let them know you are making a note for their teacher, and you want to include good things about them. Write the note at the end of the day. If the "heroes" in the class are good, rule-obeying students, you will generally find that all the class will follow. If the opposite is true, then you will find yourself in constant warfare all day. You may want to march a few of the ring leaders over to a fellow teacher for part of a class hour in order to remove the leadership and enable you to reestablish control.

As the day progresses, check off the things completed on the lesson plan and leave notes about the accomplishments of the day. Also, leave information about any difficult problems. The regular teacher may want to deal with them, and you might be called to substitute there again. Perform your duties gladly and do your best, as you would want another teacher to do for you in the same circumstance. ("Whatsoever ye would that men should do to you, do ye even so to them." Matthew 7:12)

You will find that some classes are well disciplined and that the teacher's plans are well organized. Such a class will not be difficult to teach. It is the other type for which you need to be prepared. It is called "winging it." Have in mind a couple of songs you could teach, a neat, catchy game, a simple art project, a brain teaser, a writing activity, or a math relay to fill in unscheduled space. Take along a couple of your favorite read-out-loud books. You will find a list of Newberry and Caldecott Award Winner books in the Appendix. Most classrooms have library books available for silent reading. That is always a constructive time filler. You may require the students to practice their handwriting skills. (A copy of printing and manuscript lettering is also included in the Appendix.)

Never try to undermine a colleague or talk unprofessionally to another teacher about how unorganized or unprepared the regular teacher seems to be. You can be certain that such information will be used again. Let your comments be positive, even if it is only about how great the green plants thrive under his care! The book of James addresses the subject of our tongues (James 1:26; James 3:5-13) and Proverbs 25:11 states, "A word fitly spoken is like apples of gold in pictures of silver." Strive to speak words that build, instead of words that tear down another person.

Many schools hire new teachers from their substitute list. The administration will be well aware of how you handle the job of substituting. If you manage well, then there will be no doubt that you could handle your own classroom. If you are looking for employment, this will be a "trial" time for you. Do not get discouraged if you have an unsuccessful day. Some days are better than others, and some classes are easier to handle than others. One thing is for certain, you will gain invaluable information and experience that cannot be bought with money or learned from a book.

3. STUDENTS' VIEW OF A SUBSTITUTE

From a student's point of view, a substitute unsettles their security. They have already figured out how far they can push their regular teacher. They feel comfortable because their teacher knows what he is doing and knows the necessary information about everything at school. He also knows their parents or can get in touch with them. "Sub" day can be a play day if students plan it right. Substitutes are usually not as strict as the regular teacher, and maybe they will never see the sub again. So, if they misbehave, who is to know? To students, substitutes are uncertain about schedules, bells, places, and rules. The students know these things so well that they have become second nature to them. They think then, "If this person is so uncertain about the schedule, then he must be uncertain about everything." Because of this logic, students tend to take advantage of you. Generally, students do not like for their classmates who misbehave to get the rest of the class in trouble. Some feel that there is extra work when a substitute is necessary, so they had just as soon he not come.

Unless you look like a recording star or resemble a famous football or baseball player, you will not have a lot of clout with students. However, they will accept a pleasant person. They expect you to be enthusiastic and self-confident. That makes them feel safe. Be glad to be there with them and enjoy the role of substituting. ("Rejoice in the Lord always: and again I say, Rejoice." Philippians 4:4)

4. TEACHER'S VIEW OF A SUBSTITUTE

For you as the regular teacher, a substitute can be a lifesaver. He takes over when you have to be absent. Learning can take place as you would direct it even though you are not there, if he does his job effectively. The day will go better for everyone if you plan well. Make certain that you prepare the following for the substitute:

1. A list of students and a seating chart.
2. A schedule of the daily activities.
3. Teaching guides and keys in a conspicuous place.
4. Lesson plans with a guide to abbreviated words.

Some teachers prefer to prepare a separate folder that would be available for a substitute at any time. The only problem with using that method alone is that there is no continuity of instruction with your regular lessons and the substitute becomes a babysitter. Of course, if you had been planning to launch helium balloons that day, it would probably be better to wait until you return. However, if the entire school will be participating, you will have to leave good plans for your substitute and hope for the best.

Planning for yourself is much easier than to plan for another person. There are so many things you do every day that have become habitual, and it is impossible to write it all down and to explain exactly how you do it; however, if you can determine about how much material the students will be able to cover and leave page numbers and concepts that need to be completed, a good sub should be able to carry out your plans. Always leave extra work and/or planned activities just in case you miscalculate. Students certainly do *not* need unscheduled time when a substitute teacher is in charge.

Make certain you indicate whether work completed by the students in your absence should be collected for you, graded by the students in class and kept, or left in a basket or folder. Answer keys should be available if you expect the sub to grade the papers. He will probably be dealing with unfamiliar material.

Discipline can be a problem for substitutes. If you have a workable system in your classroom (such as leaving names on the board, subtracting activity points, or checks by names), provide this helpful information. Make certain that the students understand that any problems the substitute refers to you will receive attention the day you return, and make certain you follow through. The day will go smoother for everyone involved if your presence is felt even though you are not there. You can never really predict your students' behavior in your absence. It is similar to raising your own children. You hope that they will behave away from home the same way you have taught them to do when they are in your presence.

The scriptures promise that if we "Correct thy son, [and] he shall give thee rest; yea, he shall give delight unto thy soul" (Proverbs 29:17). The goal of discipline is to produce self-disciplined students, and they need to understand that we are instructed in many instances in God's word about the undisciplined person. ("He that hath no rule over his own spirit is like a city that is broken down, and without walls" [Proverbs 25:28]. Also, Proverbs 20:11, "Even a child is known by his doings, whether his work be pure, and whether it be right.")

If you expect good behavior, students will usually live up to your expectations. If you find a sub who works well with you and your students, it is a good idea to ask for him again. Your being away is not quite so upsetting to their routine if they are accustomed to a certain substitute.

Teachers depend upon them. Students generally dislike them. Schools could not continue without them. There should be extra rewards for the special persons called "substitutes."

Chapter Thirteen

Professional Growth

A principal once remarked that he preferred teachers who had taught from one to five years. It seems, he said, that teachers tend to get set in their ways and mold. It takes effort to keep your teaching alive and interesting. Teachers really should get better with age—not moldy!

How can a teacher keep from molding? By refraining from and refusing to become stale. The "ho-hums" and the "hum-drums" may hit you, and you may be tempted to become draggy and boring. No one has to tell the parents, colleagues, principals, and students because they probably recognized the mold before you did.

Ideas that work with one group may fall flat with another. However, here are some strategies that will help you to maintain the crispness and enthusiasm of a first year teacher.

1. ASK FOR ASSISTANCE

Each fall, as you enter the names of the students in your roll book, pray for all of them and ask God to help you take them as far as they are capable of going this year. Many promises are given in the Bible about receiving if we ask and if we meet the conditions. (Matthew 7:7; John 14:14; John 15:7.) Remember that each child is just as important to their parents as your own children are or will be to you. Research has shown that your expectation of them makes a difference. They tend to live up to what you expect from them.

2. PROVIDE A THEME

Perhaps you might want a theme that would work well with the age group that you teach. One teacher used rainbows, another an underwater theme, and another used a western theme. Everything can be decorated with the theme idea in mind. For example, for the western theme, attendance is kept by using stampeding horses with students' names on them. Student helpers are indicated by boots with their names on them stuck in cowboy hats stapled to the bulletin board with the job to be done written on the hat. Best citizens are listed on a "wanted alive" poster.

3. THINK BEFORE PLANNING

Before your plans are written down, spend time thinking through your lessons. Planning can take place while you are driving the car, doing housework, or standing in line for checkout at the grocery store. Constantly question: "How can I do this lesson differently?" Or, "What would make this difficult task more fun?" Have activities, projects, plays, and lessons thought through in your mind long before you write them down in your plan book or attempt to carry them out. Think through the steps of motivation, teaching the lesson, drill, and closure or review of the lesson.

4. USE MUSIC

Taking only five minutes a day, your students can learn a song about the scriptures, the flag, or any other worthwhile subject. Put the words on a chalkboard, bulletin board, or poster and sing it everyday. By the end of the year, they can sing scripture songs and other songs such as "America," "The Star Spangled Banner," and "God Bless America."

After sitting for prolonged periods, sing an exercise song or camp song to permit them to stretch or to make the transition from one activity to another.

5. GIVE PRAISE

Say to your students, "How glad I am to have you in my class!", or "You make me so happy when you work well together!" Always complaining and grumbling at the students is a sure sign of becoming stale. Freshen your outlook by constantly reminding yourself to be joyful.

6. PLAN FOR INCLEMENT WEATHER

In preparation for recess time that has to be spent inside because of the weather, planning should be done to avoid chaos. One idea is to use ten sets of jacks and let them practice in groups of three or four on the floor in the classroom, or use chess sets. During the longest periods of inclement weather, tournament brackets can be made and play-offs between pairs of children can be planned. Enthusiasm will be exhibited, eye-hand coordination developed, and Christian characteristics such as fairness and kindness can be taught. A gigantic plus is that the students will look forward to days spent inside.

7. TAKE ADVANTAGE OF OPPORTUNITIES

There are professional organizations for teachers in each state, and there are also Christian teacher organizations. Attend some of the meetings and determine whether or not the organization could benefit you. Then choose the one(s) to join.

Take advantage of the in-service seminars offered and determine to learn new ideas and approaches for teaching. Some school districts require teachers to attend certain in-service programs. Attend with the right attitude and with eagerness to improve your teaching.

There are numerous magazines that are published monthly that offer the teacher different ideas for bulletin boards, art, and other areas of the curriculum. You may find them available at a college library or you may subscribe to them yourself. Also, there are book clubs available for teachers, or you may check out books from the nearest college library that would provide new and fresh ideas for your classroom.

8. ANTICIPATE TOMORROW

Ask yourself what you can do to make the next day at school fun. Sometimes changing the regular school routine can help you and the students to anticipate the next school day. For example, give a play, have those who follow certain directions get a prize from the grab bag (filled with odds and ends from home), or make homemade ice cream. When the teacher anticipates the day, so will the children.

There is no need to get moldy in your teaching. Stay fresh and change when change would be beneficial. Try something each school year that you have never tried before. Keep abreast of the research being done in your field by subscribing to and reading professional journals. Read books and articles that teachers are writing about ideas and activities that work for them. Attend workshops and professional growth days with an open mind. Teachers may not all become great, but they all have the opportunity to inspire someone else to be. We are admonished in the scriptures to be "not slothful in business; fervent in spirit; serving the Lord" (Romans 12:11). This responsibility seems to be worth fighting the mold!

Chapter Fourteen

Teacher Feedback

Who pats the teacher's back and tells him how much his work is appreciated? Hardly anyone will until retirement, when usually a farewell party is given. For some that is too long to wait, especially for new teachers who need encouragement. Teachers may wonder how parents and the principal are viewing their work. Does the principal like their methods of teaching, and do the students really retain and transfer the material being taught? Many times the feedback teachers receive is negative, and the teacher may feel that everything he does goes unseen except the mistakes he has made.

Those available to give feedback to the teacher include the following groups.

1. PARENTS

Parents tend either to criticize teachers or try to please them. Some do pat teachers on the back and praise them for a job well done. Others feel that they really do not know enough about education to judge one way or another.

2. STUDENTS

Feedback from younger students (K-3) is usually instant and spontaneous. If you have been the model before them that God intended you to be, they will respond positively to your teaching. They usually like school and think their teacher is wonderful. As students mature, the peer group is so important that the teacher begins to fade somewhat. They expect you to do your job and feedback becomes less frequent.

3. PRINCIPALS

Principals tend to become involved in many important tasks that are necessary for the successful operation of a school. There is little time for them to assist teachers. There is usually little time available for them to visit individual classes except once or twice during the year. During those visits, a yearly check-list is usually filled out to indicate the teacher's strengths and weaknesses. It should be an encouragement for the teacher, but often he feels discouraged about his deficiencies.

4. COLLEAGUES

Some teachers tend to degrade the successes of fellow teachers instead of supporting them. It is so easy to see mistakes of others and to excuse the same mistakes (or worse ones) in ourselves (Luke 7:41).

Another teacher may feel threatened or inadequate because he did not think of an idea or activity first. If a teacher is recognized for bulletin board displays or beautiful art projects, rumors may begin circulating about how poorly he disciplines! The scriptures instruct us to: "Be kindly affectioned one to another with brotherly love; in honour preferring one another" (Romans 12:10). Why not make a practice of complimenting at least one colleague every day?

You may have to think of ways to produce feedback. When you see the principal close by, invite him into your room to see your latest project or observe an activity or lesson in which the students are successful. Most principals would appreciate such an invitation.

Select a fellow teacher and stop by his room at a convenient moment. Ask, "What are you doing this week that works?" or "What can you share with me today that might be exciting for my students also?" Pat him on the back and admire his work. Even if he just put up a new bulletin board or straightened his room, it's encouraging when someone else cares and appreciates the effort.

Give a program and invite the parents to see the children perform. Most parents will be appreciative of the time you have spent with their child. Perhaps one might say, "You have done such a good job with my son that I want you to teach my daughter." What a compliment! Take it as a pat on the back.

Business employees get monetary bonuses for a job well done. Insurance companies give complimentary gifts and trips to top salesmen. Farmers receive an abundant yield from their crops if they toil faithfully and the weather is favorable. Military personnel receive complimentary fitness reports and medals when they accomplish their work successfully. Students receive high marks for academic achievement. Teachers, many times, have to settle for a small note at the bottom of a paper! "I LOVE YOU. You are the best teacher in the world!"

Be conscientious about your responsibilities and work hard. Someone *will* notice. Having your back patted occasionally will help your reservoir not to run dry, and—hopefully—you will not be tempted to give up your calling. Teachers doing an outstanding job have been known to quit because no one gave them the encouragement they needed.

As a Christian, our strength and encouragement comes from the source of all strength. There are numerous scriptures about strength, one of which is Psalm 28:78, "The Lord is my strength and my shield: my heart trusted in Him, and I am helped: therefore my heart greatly rejoiceth: and with my song will I praise Him. The Lord is their strength, and He is the saving strength of His anointed."

A favorite scriptural promise of one super Christian teacher is Isaiah 58:10,11: "And if thou draw out thy soul to the hungry, and satisfy the afflicted soul;. . . the Lord shall guide thee continually, and satisfy thy soul in drought, and make fat thy bones: and thou shalt be like a watered garden, and like a spring of water, whose waters fail not." Daily strength can be yours through reading such scriptures or calling them to mind. His strength can be yours as you daily rely on the Master Teacher, and you will be able to teach with joy!

Chapter Fifteen

Teachers Who Burn Out

The first year of teaching is probably the most difficult for any teacher. Every disease and illness that elementary age children experience is usually passed on to the beginning teacher. There is much information to assimilate and equipment with which to become familiar. The teacher also finds out who is a good listener and an encourager among the staff and faculty. He learns the principal's toleration level on varied issues and activities. There are specifics about the school and community that are important for him to know. During the first year the teacher attempts to organize all the information that is being given and attempts to avoid confusion. However, usually some of the specifics will be overlooked, and a new faculty member will find himself in chaos. Longstanding traditions that seem to exist may add to his misunderstanding. You will not be the first new teacher who sheds tears while settling into your role.

A diary kept during the first year would be interesting to read later. The children's comments and circumstances that you encounter will be unforgettable. Experience will be a good teacher, and you will get plenty the first year! Also remember that every time a teacher transfers to a different school, state, or grade level, it is like starting all over again.

Many teachers who survive the first year do not continue to teach until retirement. The problem of teacher retention is being considered today by educators in order to keep effective teachers longer. There are many reasons why teachers leave their careers early. These reasons include:

1. HOMEWORK

Teachers could easily spend all their time out of the classroom on school work. There are stacks and tons of papers to grade, planning and preparing of lessons to complete, and bulletin boards to dress. Parents need to be informed, and students need assistance outside of class.

Some leave their calling because they have been pressured into giving up extra activities that they enjoy. These may include giving up valuable time they formerly spent with their families, or giving up entertaining or visiting friends outside their profession. Their world becomes smaller and smaller as they do nothing but school work, and they nearly dry up on the vine. Spending all of your extra time working for the school is not healthy. A teacher needs to be involved in other activities. As you take refreshment away from your duties, you will be better prepared to plunge in again later. Jesus pictured us as branches and Himself as the vine. Considering all our relationships, our relationship with Him is the most vital.

There are times when you have to consider duties other than school work because they are necessary. However, reduce your load by working vigorously while you are at school. This can be enhanced by spot checking the children's written work. Walk around your classroom and either grade their work as they finish or put a stamp, check, or comment on their paper as they complete them. Work can be accomplished as a class, and then the assignment will not need correcting. Many teachers let students grade some of their own practice work or exchange with a neighbor. Generally, teachers are expected to record an average of two grades a week for each subject taught. Mountains of paper work can be successfully eliminated if you plan carefully.

The amount of work that you take home should be limited because you will quickly tire of the extra load. You cannot afford to spend all your breathing time on homework. You'll suffocate.

2. DISCIPLINE

During the pre-service training years, many education students have the impression that when lessons are planned well and classes are made challenging, the children will be so engrossed in learning that they will not have time to misbehave. Many teachers in training apparently have the notion that if children *do* misbehave, then it is because their lessons are not properly organized. In reality, getting the children's attention and keeping it is the most difficult assignment of teaching. Challenging and well-planned lessons will aid the teacher in student behavior, but will not guarantee thirty well-disciplined students.

Many beginning teachers are surprised at the amount of energy and time required for keeping order in the classroom. When you are instructing, it is necessary to have the students' attention. Also remember that being able to conduct an orderly class is usually a high priority on the principal's checklist.

There are districts that have high rates of teacher abuses reported. Even in the best of situations, there are teachers who feel that disciplining children is too time consuming and not worth the effort. They find other professions more appealing where they face less of these kinds of frustrations.

3. BOREDOM

Teaching includes repetition and drill. Repeating information day after day and year after year could become monotonous. Some teachers become bored with the process and want to find more challenging material. Worse still are the ones who stay in the teaching profession anyway! They continue to bore children with boring material using a boring style. The Lord has spoken to us about how we are to approach our work, "And whatsoever ye do, do it heartily, as to the Lord, and not unto men" (Colossians 3:23). Accomplishing your work in the classroom in that manner will lead to joyous teaching.

There are ways to prevent boredom that have been profitable for other teachers. These include changing grade levels every few years or changing locations. Take an additional course or a workshop to receive fresh ideas. Keep spice in your teaching by varying approaches. Plan to do some activities or lessons with your class that are special interests of yours and into which you can get involved emotionally.

Getting into a rut is easier than you think, and staying there is easier than learning something new and different. Staying there tends to damage and stifle your enthusiasm and creativity.

4. PRESSURES

Directives from principals, expectations from parents, pulsating energy from students, and/or the responsibility felt from within have often overwhelmed those who have decided to leave the classroom.

Perhaps the best solution is starting early to prevent these situations from becoming overpowering to you. There is a verse that is a promise to us: "There hath no temptation taken you but such as is common to man: but God is faithful, who will not permit you to be tempted above that you are able, but will, with the temptation, also make a way to escape, that you may be able to bear it" (I Corinthians 10:13). As Christians, we can be assured that no test or trial will be too great for us if we are relying on God to provide a way of escape, and if we are willing to accept the way of escape He provides. If teaching does seem too difficult, God may be providing you another place of service. Take advantage of the opportunity because no job is worth taking tranquilizers in order to cope with the pressures.

5. INCOME

Teachers' salaries are not competitive with many other professions. Skilled laborers who do not have college degrees earn more money per hour. Those teachers who support a family usually seek for employment through the summer months.

There is little chance that teachers' salaries will ever become competitive. Teachers who are mothers have the advantage of having hours at school similar to their children, and of having the same vacations. Those who are called to this profession must consider the rewards of having influence on the lives of tomorrow's citizens and of being able to use their talents and gifts to the fullest extent. For some, this is not enough and they leave the profession and find a more profitable occupation.

Man's insatiable desire for riches is addressed numerous times in the scriptures. God made us and knows us. I Timothy 6:10 states that "The *love* of money is the root of all evil." When our Lord was here on earth, He stressed that our treasures are to be laid up in heaven, not on earth. Jeremiah 9:23, 24 says, "Thus saith the Lord, Let not the wise man glory in his wisdom, neither let the mighty man glory in his might, let not the rich man glory in his riches: But let him that glorieth glory in this, that he understandeth and knoweth me, that I am the Lord which exercise lovingkindness, judgment, and righteousness, in the earth: for in these things I delight, saith the Lord." We are also given a promise that Christian teachers should keep in mind: "I have been young, and now am old; yet have I not seen the righteous forsaken, nor His seed begging bread" (Psalm 37:25). Christian teachers may not become rich, but God's Word states that because we are His, we will never be hungry.

6. EXPECTATIONS

Some may have such high expectations about teaching that they become disillusioned. If you expect to motivate and challenge every student to his fullest capacity during the school year, you are probably too idealistic. In education that is a worthy goal, but in reality it is quite difficult. Because students are not mature, their interests are diverse, learning disabilities are present, and problems at home are prevalent, teachers face difficult challenges every year.

At times you may feel that you are only able to motivate a few and that your struggle is uphill and into the wind. Be realistic in setting goals for the year. Picture yourself as a steady, slow, dependable, lifetime star instead of a gigantic nova—a bright blast that burns out too quickly.

If you persevere in the classroom, there are rewards that will be yours. If you allow God to love through you and reach out to the lovable and unlovable, endure through the hardships, and maintain a burning desire to serve, you will be blessed. Your contribution will be priceless, and you will be wealthy because of the investment you have made in the lives of the children you teach. Each time one of them is successful, you get a return on your investment. Your harvest will be bountiful every time one comes to you with thanks or praise for the time, energy, and talent you have spent assisting in his education.

Chapter Sixteen

Joyful Teaching

Throughout this book the importance of being joyful as you accomplish the task of teaching has been emphasized. Paul instructs in Philippians 4:4 to "Rejoice in the Lord alway; and again I say, rejoice." That's not *humanly* possible, but with God's help, we can rejoice, even in the midst of calamity. If problems can be viewed as challenges, and if you pray "with thanksgiving," then "the peace of God which passeth all understanding shall keep your hearts and minds through Christ Jesus" (Philippians 4:6, 7).

As you teach you will have trials. Life is full of problem-solving, but you would have had problems in any other career you might have chosen. Therefore, remember all of the reasons why you considered teaching as your life's goal and why teaching is important.

1. God's call—"And He gave some...teachers" (Ephesians 4:11).
2. Love for children—"And whoso shall receive one such little child in my name receiveth me" (Matthew 18:5).
3. Influence on students—"A pupil is not above his teacher, but everyone, after he has been fully trained will be like his teacher" (Luke 6:40).

Also consider the many passages in the Bible about rejoicing and being joyful. Some of them from Psalms include:

1. "But let all those that put their trust in thee REJOICE; let them ever shout for JOY, because thou defendest them: let them also that love thy name be JOYFUL in thee" (Psalm 5:11).
2. "I will be glad and REJOICE in thee: I will sing praise to thy name, O thou Most High" (Psalm 9:2).
3. "Thou wilt shew me the path of life: in thy presence is fulness of JOY; at thy right hand there are pleasures for evermore" (Psalm 16:11).
4. "Be glad in the Lord, and REJOICE, ye righteous: and shout for JOY, all ye that are upright in heart" (Psalm 32:11).
5. "For our heart shall REJOICE in him, because we have trusted in his holy name" (Psalm 33:21).
6. "Let them shout for JOY, and be glad, that favour my righteous cause: yea, let them say continually, Let the Lord be magnified, which hath pleasure

in the prosperity of his servant'' (Psalm 35:27).

7. ''Let all those that seek thee REJOICE and be glad in thee'' (Psalm 70:4a).

8. ''My lips shall greatly REJOICE when I sing unto thee; and my soul, which thou has redeemed'' (Psalm 71:23).

9. ''They that sow in tears shall reap with JOY'' (Psalms 126:5).

10. ''Let thy priests be clothed with righteousness; and let thy saints shout for JOY'' (Psalms 132:9).

In Galatians 5:22 Paul lists the fruits of the spirit that Christians should demonstrate in their lives. Of course, joy is one of those fruits: ''But the fruit of the spirit is love, JOY, peace, longsuffering, gentleness, goodness, faith. . . .''

In fact, as a Christian our joy should not depend on any outward circumstances. Our joy depends on our relationship with the living Lord! Habakkuk 3:17-19a records how we should react in times of calamity: ''Although the fig tree shall not blossom, neither shall fruit be in the vines; the labour of the olive shall fail, and the fields shall yield no meat; the flock shall be cut off from the fold, and there shall be no herd in the stalls: Yet I will REJOICE in the Lord, I will JOY in the God of my salvation. The Lord God is my strength. . . .''

Therefore, as you teach, determine in your mind and heart to do so with joy!

Appendix

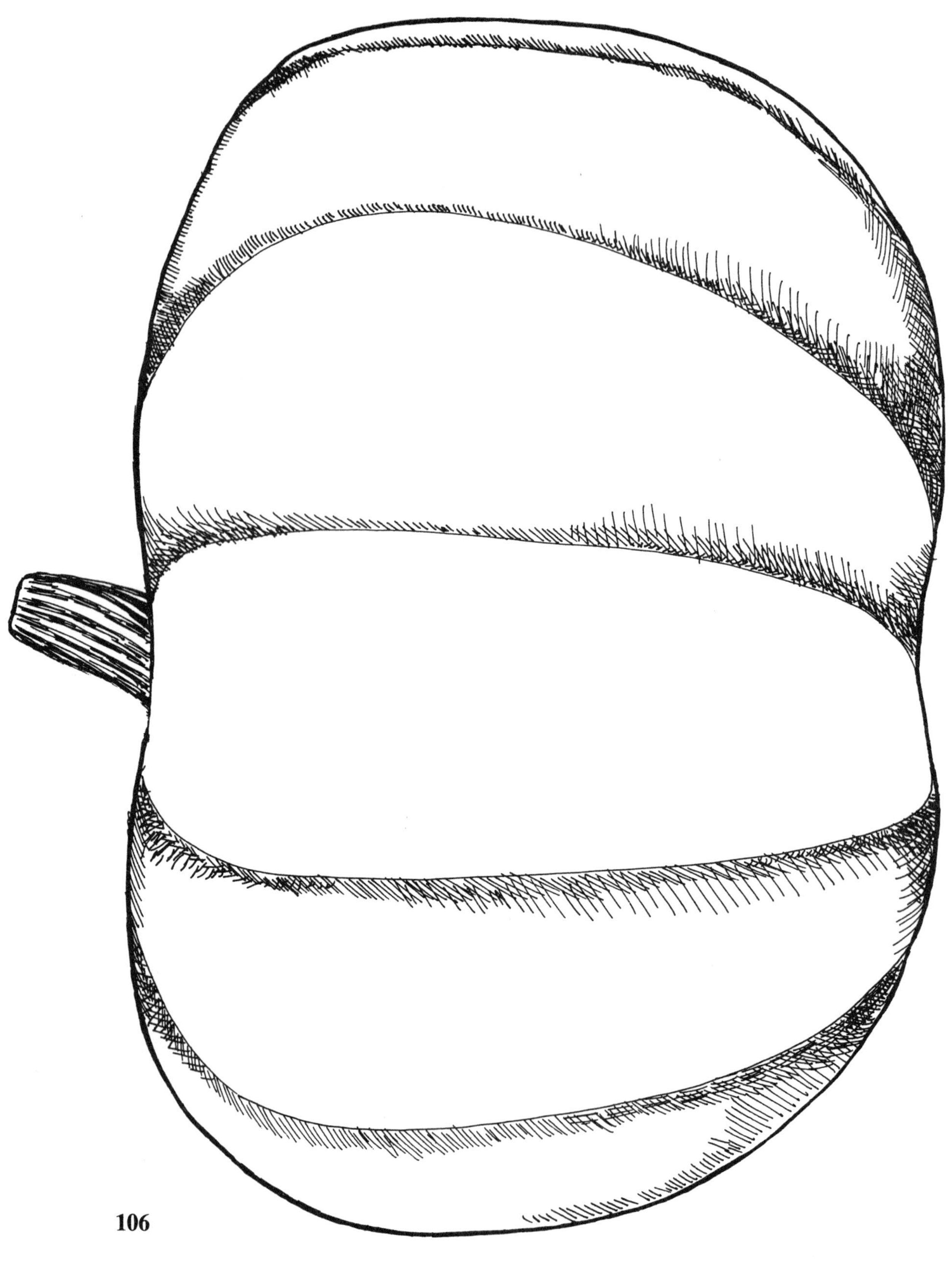

A TIME TO GIVE THANKS

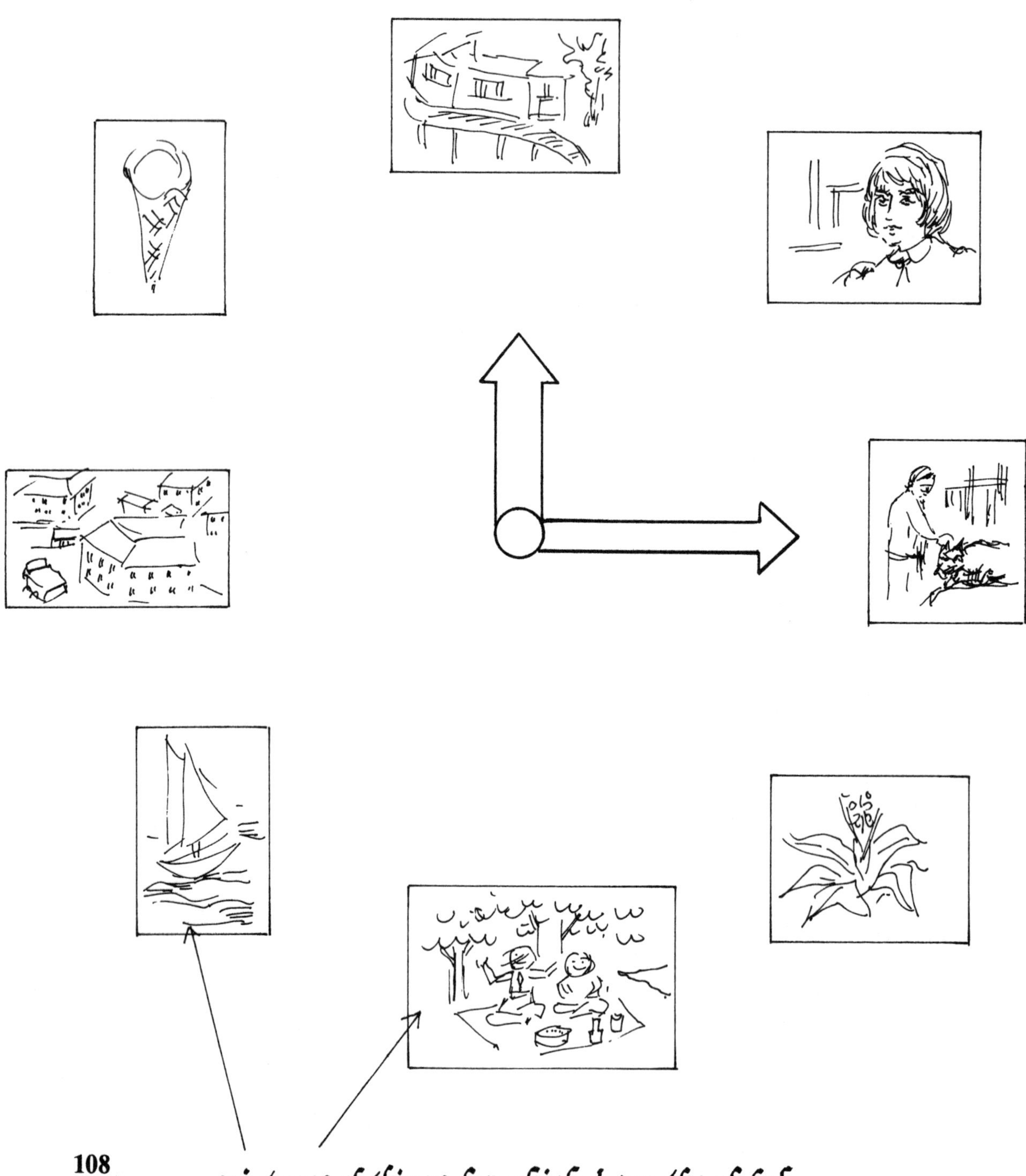

pictures of things for which I am thankful

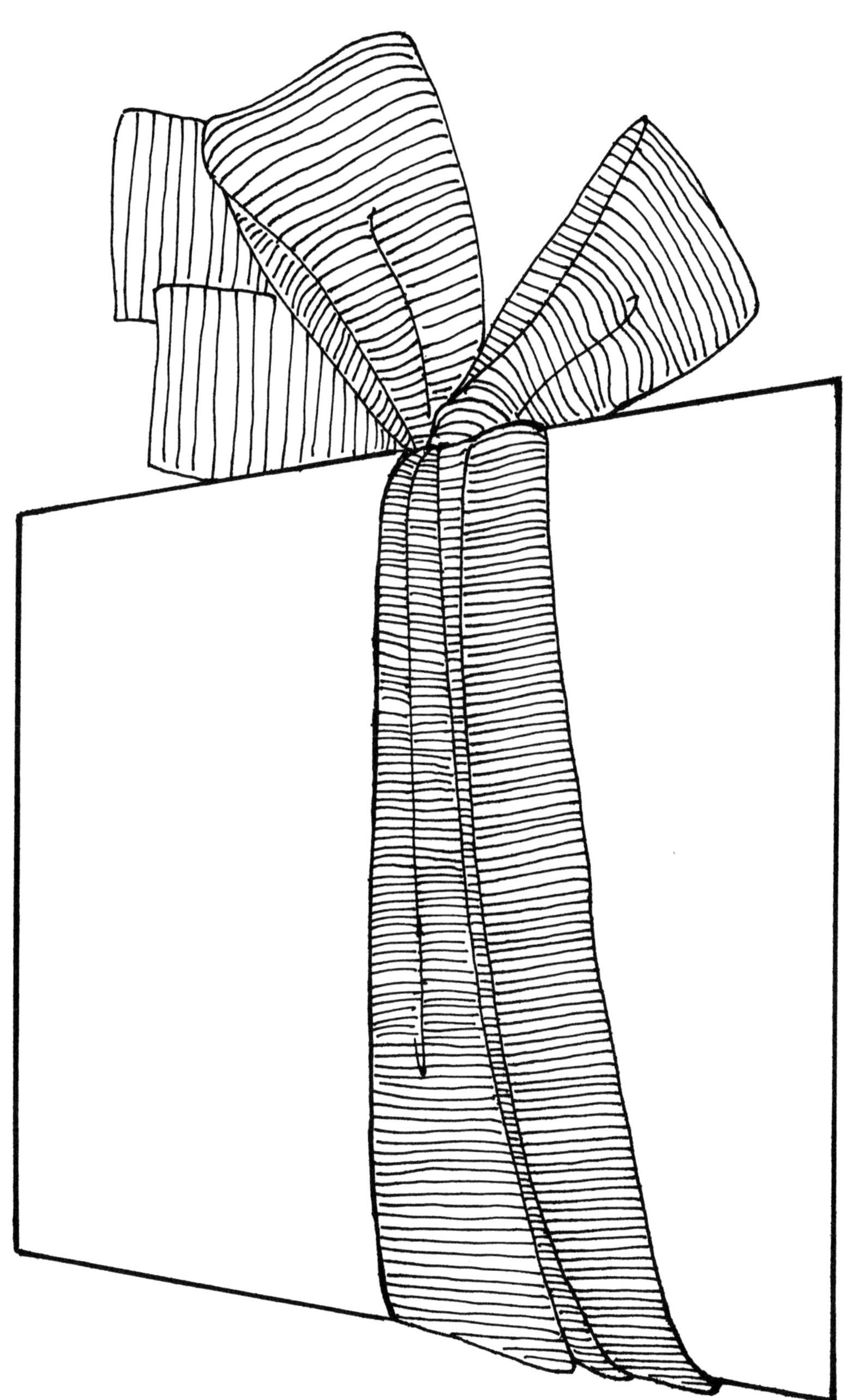

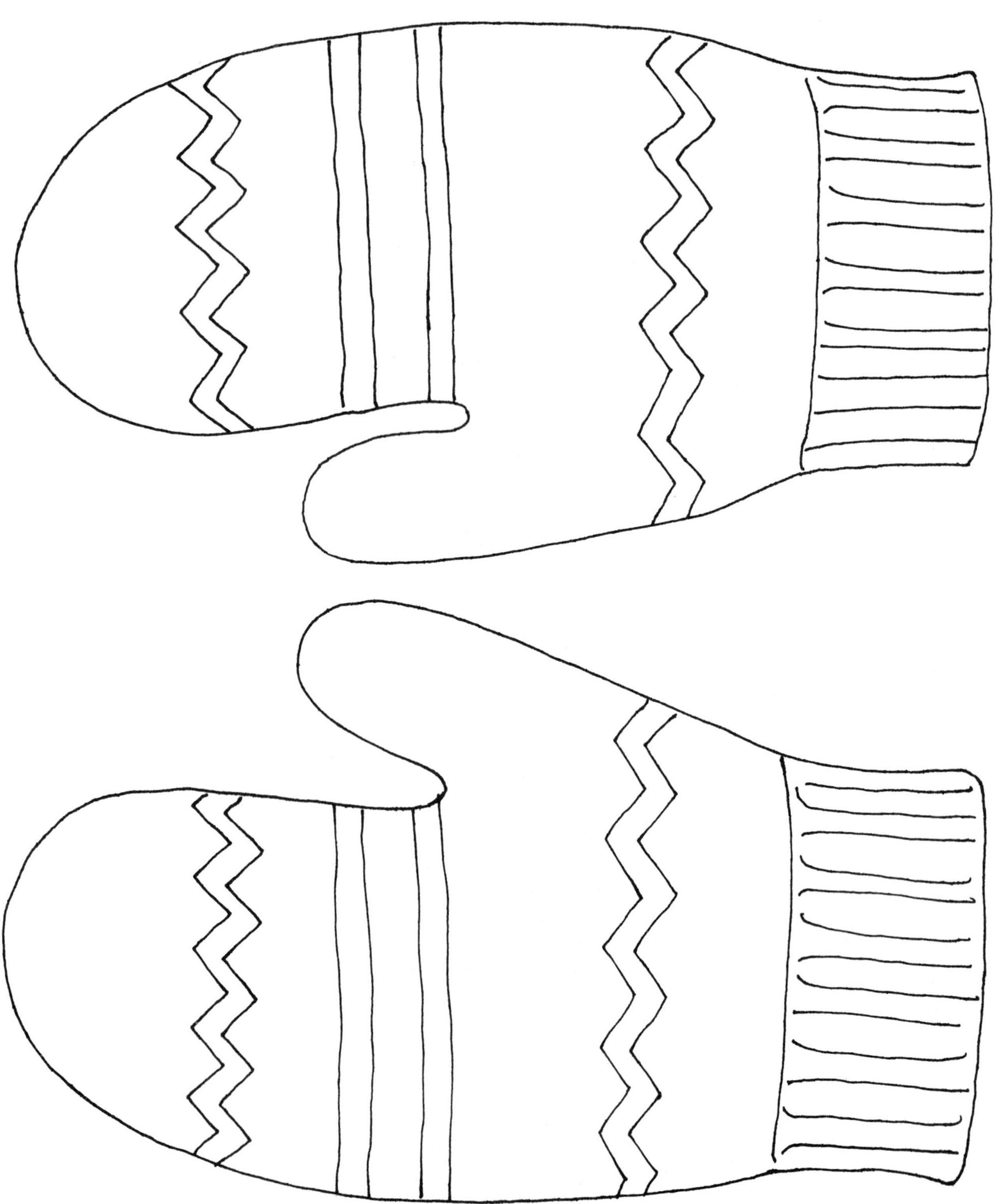

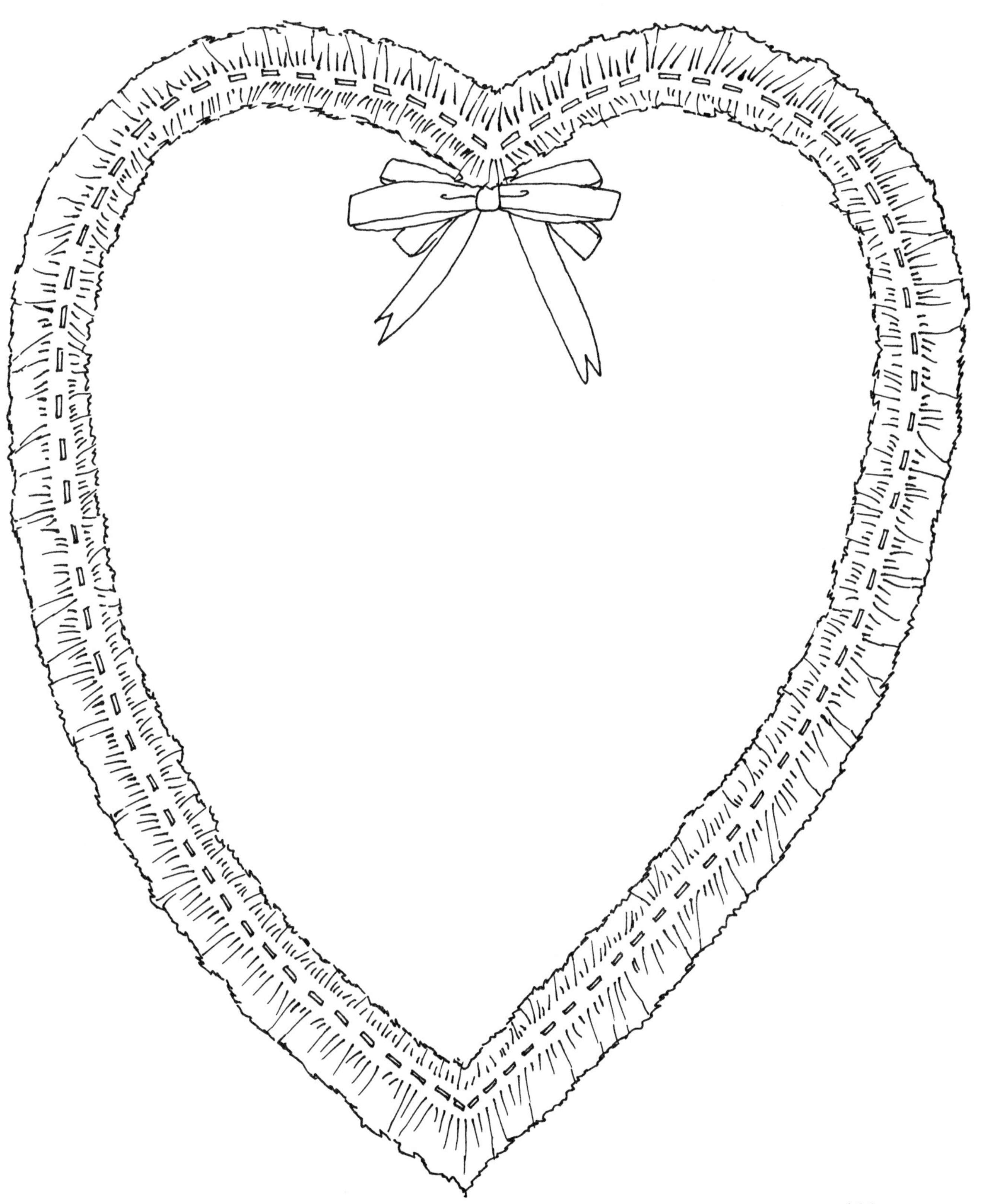

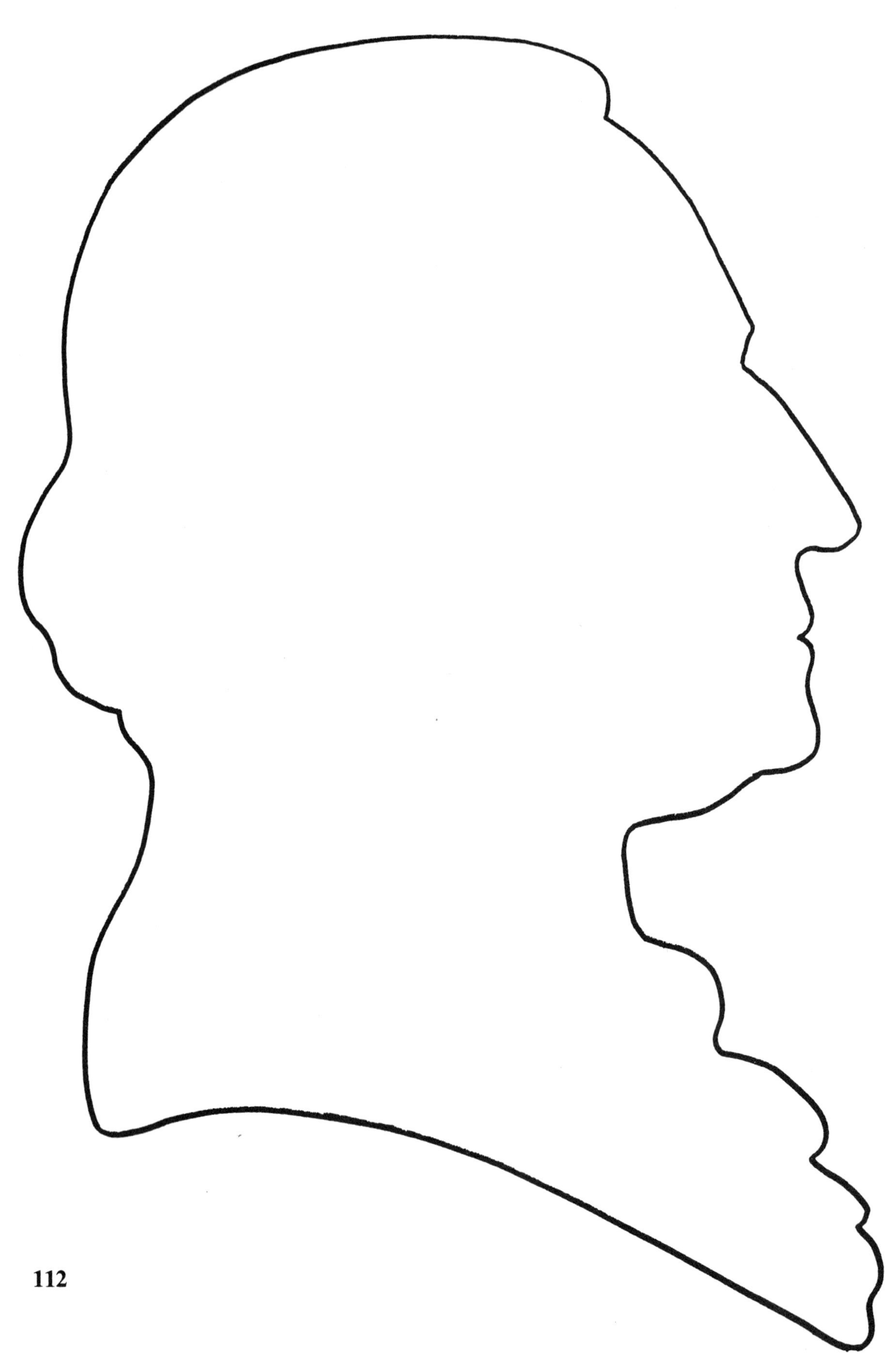

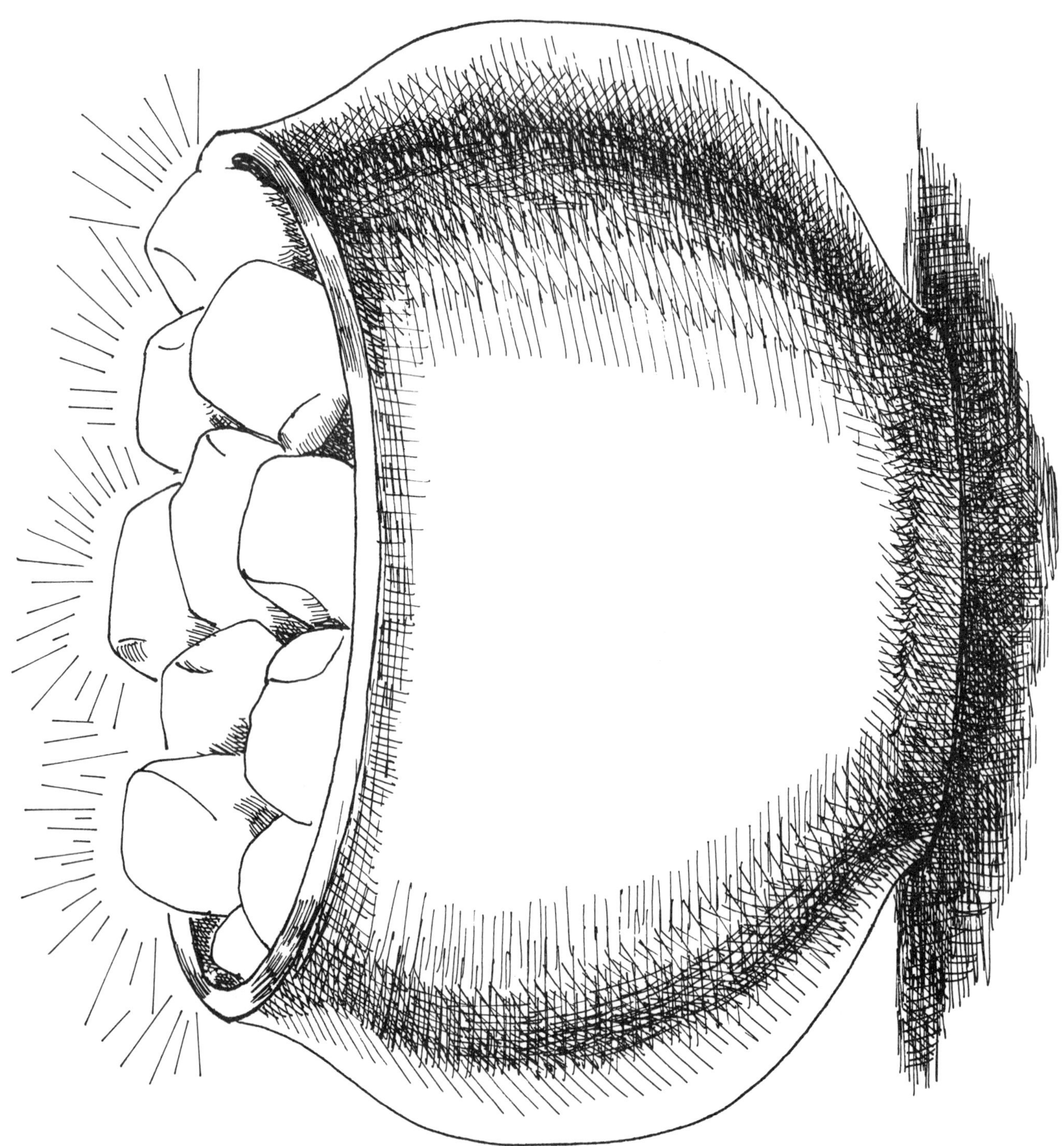

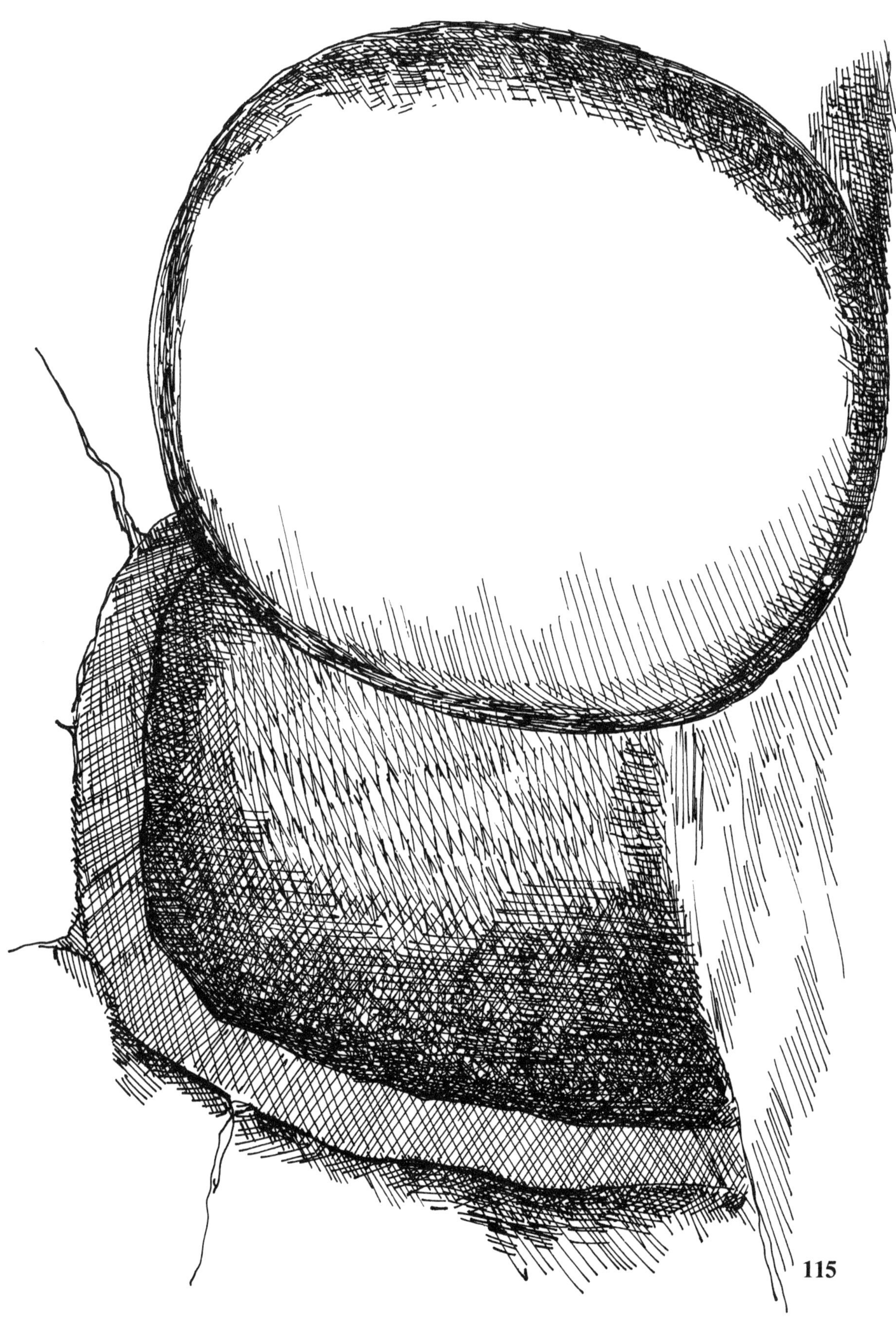

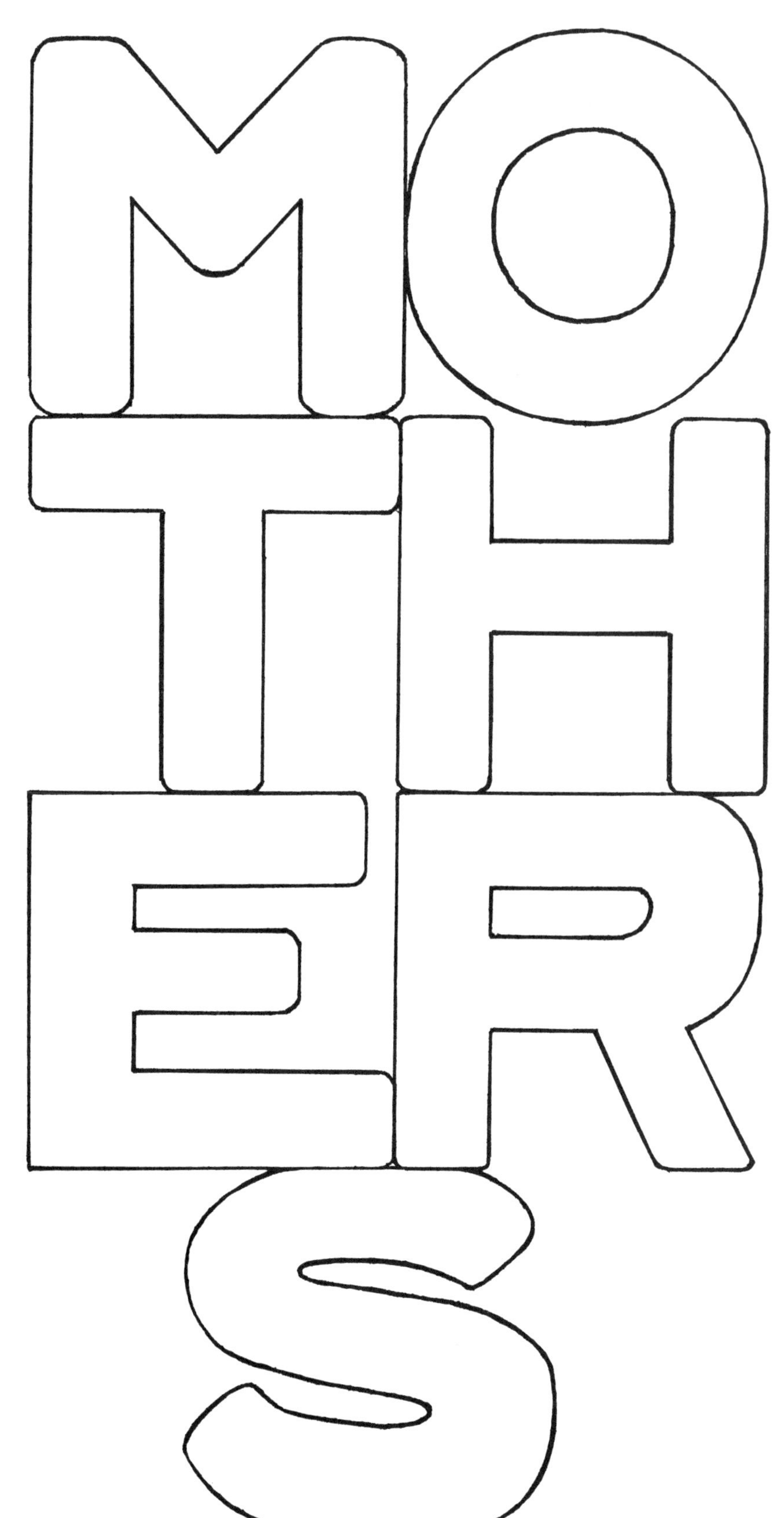
MO
TH
ER
S

Aa Bb Cc Dd Ee Ff
Gg Hh Ii Jj Kk Ll Mm
Nn Oo Pp Qq Rr Ss
Tt Uu Vv Ww Xx Yy Zz
1 2 3 4 5 6 7 8 9 0 ? ; :

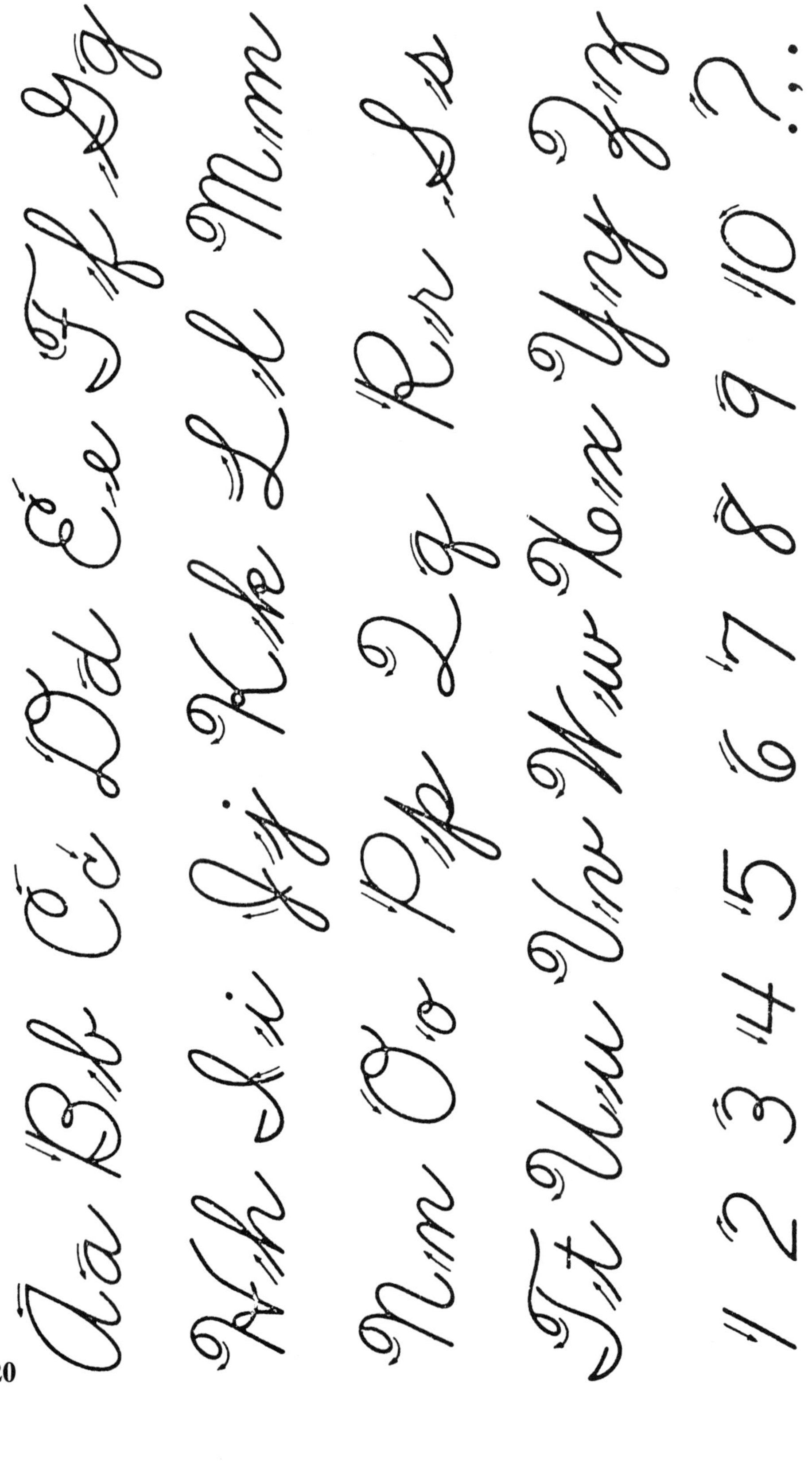

Aa Bb Cc Dd Ee Ff Gg

Hh Ii Jj Kk Ll Mm

Nn Oo Pp Qq Rr Ss

Tt Uu Vv Ww Xx Yy Zz

1 2 3 4 5 6 7 8 9 10 ? . , .

Bibliography

An awards committee of the American Library Association's Children's Services Division gives two awards annually in the area of children's literature. Since 1922 the Newberry Award has been given to the author of the most distinguished contribution of literature for children published in the United States during the preceding year. Beginning in 1938, the illustrator of the most distinguished picture book for children has been recognized by receiving the Caldecott Award. The following annotated bibliography includes those books which, in my opinion, can be adapted to the Christian classroom.

Newberry Medal Award Books

Angeli, Marguerite. *The Door in the Wall.* New York: Doubleday and Company, Inc., 1949.

The drama and pageantry of medieval life is included, plus the simple realism of the common-folk ways. The story is about Robin who was crippled enroute to serve as a page to the castle in the north. (4-6)

Armstrong, William. *Sounder.* New York: Harper and Row Publishers, 1969.

Sounder, a great coon dog, and his black master live and die through hard times while the boy who loves them both has to bear his sorrow like a man. (4-6)

Blos, Joan. *A Gathering of Days: A New England Girl's Journal 1830-32.* New York: Charles Scribner's Sons, 1979.

The hardships and tranquility of the early American farm life is depicted in this diary by a girl in New England. (4-6)

Brink, Carol Ryrie. *Caddie Woodlawn.* New York: Macmillan, 1935.

A book written about life during early America which depicts Caddie's pioneer childhood. (4-6)

Daugherty, James. *Daniel Boone.* New York: The Viking Press, 1939.

Daniel Boone's story of settling the West and the struggles between the Indians and white men.

DeJong, Meindert. *The Wheel on the School.* New York: Harper and Row, 1954.

Six Dutch children in a fishing village have to overcome many obstacles to get storks to come and build nests. (3-6)

Enright, Elizabeth. *Thimble Summer.* New York: Holt, Rinehart and Winston, 1938.

A richly descriptive story of a little girl's summer which includes being locked in a library. (4-6)

Estes, Eleanor. *Ginger Pye.* New York: Harcourt, Brace and World, Inc., 1951.

A family story about the Pyes and their dog, Ginger. (4-6)

Fried, Rachel. *Hitty, Her First Hundred Years.* New York: Macmillan Publishing Co., Inc., 1930.

A doll, Hitty, was carved from a piece of white ash. She tells of her exciting and instructive memoirs. (4-6)

Gray, Elizabeth. *Adam of the Road.* New York: Viking Press, 1942.

An eleven-year-old travels and hunts for his stolen dog and lost father during 13th Century England. (5-6)

Latham, Jean. *Carry On Mr. Bowditch.* Boston: Houghton-Mifflin Company, 1955.

A sailor who is good in mathematics tells of his adventures and sorrows. (4-6)

Lawson, Robert. *Robert Hill.* New York: The Viking Press, 1944.

Twelve adventures narrated by animals are told about a rabbit, Georgie, and his family and friends. (K-3)

Lenski, Lori. *Strawberry Girl.* Philadelphia: J. B. Lippincott and Company, 1973.

Two Florida families struggle through their differences and learn to help each other. (4-6)

Meigs, Cornelia. *Invincible Louisa.* Boston: Little, Brown and Company, 1933.

Louisa May Alcott and her eventful career is vividly portrayed in this book. (5-6)

O'Dell, Scott. *Island of the Blue Dolphins.* New York: Dell Publishing Company, 1960.

A young Indian girl is left behind on an island where her people once lived. She has to take care of herself while surviving alone. (4-6)

Sawyer, Ruth. *Roller Skates.* New York: The Viking Press, 1936.

Lucinda has many experiences while she is ten, especially on roller skates. (3-6)

Sorensen, Virginia. *Miracles on Maple Hill.* New York: Harcourt, Brace and World, Inc., 1956.

Marly and his family discover miracles at the farmhouse on Maple Hill. (3-6)

Speare, Elizabeth. *The Bronze Bow.* New York: Houghton Books, 1962.

The story takes place during the time of Jesus and the Roman occupation of Israel. Many of the major characters' lives become changed after they see Jesus and the special miracles He performs. (4-6)

Taylor, Mildred. *Roll of Thunder, Hear My Cry.* New York: The Dial Press, 1976.

Set in Mississippi at the height of the Depression, this is the story of a black family's struggle to maintain their integrity, pride, and independence. (4-6)

Caldecott Medal Award Books

Burton, Virginia. *Little House.* Boston: Houghton Mifflin Company, 1942.

The little house experiences the seasons and many changes during the years. (K-3)

Chaucer, Geoffrey. *Chanticleer and the Fox.* New York: Thomas Crowell Co., 1958.

A story about a proud rooster and a wily fox who flattered him is told from one of the *Canterbury Tales.* (2-4)

D'Aulaire, Ingri and Edgar. *Abraham Lincoln.* New York: Doubleday Company, 1939.

Lincoln's life from birth to the Civil War is told through this book. (3-4)

Field, Rachel. *Prayer for a Child.* New York: The Macmillan Company, 1944.

A child's prayer that is illustrated. (K-1)

Hader, Berta and Elmer. *The Big Snow.* New York: Collier Books, 1948.

The snow came and the people who lived in the stone house fed the animals during the winter. (K-3)

Hall, Donald. *Ox Cart Man.* New York: Viking Press, 1979.

A story of a farmer and his family during harvest time. (1-3)

Hogrogian, Nonny. *One Fine Day.* New York: Collier Books, 1971.

A cumulative tale of a fox who lost his tail to an old farm woman and spent the day bargaining to get it back. (K-2)

Keats, Eza Jack. *The Snowy Day.* New York: The Viking Press, 1962.

Peter woke up to find a snowy day. He played all day and again the next day in the snow. (K-1)

Lawson, Robert. *They Were Strong and Good.* New York: The Viking Press, 1940.

The author wrote about his parents and grandparents. (1-3)

MacDonald, Golden. *The Little Island.* New York: Doubleday and Company, Inc., 1946.

A little island experiences the seasons and many animals. (K-2)

McCloskey, Robert. *Make Way for Ducklings.* New York: Doubleday and Company, Inc., 1946.

A delightful story about a family of ducks. (K-2)

McCloskey, Robert. *Time of Wonder.* New York: Viking Press, 1957.

The story of the author's Maine Island home. (K-3)

Petersham, Maud and Miska. *The Rooster Crows.* New York: Collier Books, 1945.

A book of American rhymes and jingles. (K-2)

Schenk de Regniers, Beatrice. *May I Bring a Friend?* New York: Atheneum, 1964.

The king and queen invite a young friend to tea and allow him to bring a friend. They all come from the zoo. (K-3)

Spier, Peter. *Noah's Ark.* New York: Doubleday Company, 1977.

A pictorial story of the flood and the animals and people saved in the ark. (K-3)

Thurber, James. *Many Moons.* New York: Harcourt, Brace and World, Inc., 1943.

The little princess wanted the moon and her father wanted to grant her that wish. (2-4)

Tresselt, Alvin. *White Snow, Bright Snow.* New York: Lothrop, Lee and Shepard Co., 1947.

The first snow flakes fall and everyone prepares for the cold weather. (K-2)

Udry, Janice. *A Tree Is Nice.* New York: Harper and Row Publishers, 1956.

This story is about trees and why we need them. (K-3)

Ward, Lynd. *The Biggest Bear.* Boston: Houghton-Mifflin Company, 1952.

A little bear grows to be very big and something has to be done with him. (K-3)

Will. *Finders Keepers.* New York: Harcourt, Brace and World, Inc., 1951.

Winkle and Nap are two dogs who found a bone. They try to find someone to tell them who should have it. (K-2)

Bible & Science Books for Children

Dinosaurs: Those Terrible Lizards
Duane T. Gish, Ph.D.
At last! A book for young people, from a creationist perspective, on those intriguing dinosaurs. No one living in the world today has ever seen a real live dinosaur—but did people of earlier times live with dinosaurs? Were dragons of ancient legends really dinosaurs? Does the Bible speak about dinosaurs? The answers are in this book! Written by Dr. Gish, noted scientist who is author of the best seller *Evolution? The Fossils Say NO!*, this book is profusely illustrated in color on beautiful 9" x 11" pages. **Cloth No. 046**

Dry Bones...and Other Fossils
Gary E. Parker, M.S., Ed.D.
Ideal for children, as well as adults. Travel with the Parker family as they spend their annual vacations hunting fossils. Written in conversational dialogue, this fascinating book explains in easy and interesting terms all about fossils...what they are, where they are found, and how they were formed. Strong evangelical emphasis. Fully illustrated in cartoons, this book is fun as well as educational. 8½" x 11". **No. 047**

Children's Travel Guide & Activities Book
Jim & Darline Robinson
A book of fascinating activities to occupy the minds of children of varying ages...whether you are actually taking the trip described, or just visiting these exciting places by way of your imagination. Games, puzzles, and Scripture exercises with a specific aim...revealing the God of creation in all the wondrous sights you can explore. This book takes you to Colorado, Utah, and New Mexico. In addition to the "fun" things for the young people, it contains helpful information for the whole family, such as facilities available at various recreation spots, etc. If you plan to visit our evolution-oriented national parks, you will want to instruct your children prior to your arrival about the scientifically accurate alternative to the story they will hear about the origins of these locations. This book is an excellent and enjoyable way to do just that. 8½" x 11". **No. 033**

What's In An Egg?
Joan Gleason Budai
Many living things get their start in the inside of an egg...and children will be intrigued to learn about what actually goes on in there! They will also gain a special appreciation of God's intricate handiwork in each of His creations. Sometimes it is difficult to explain to a child how life begins. Through the use of pictures and plain talk, this book tells them the story from "egg" to actual birth. **No. 185**

Adventures at Mountain Haven (Stubby Stories No. 1)
Lloyd Fezler
Adventures at Mountain Haven is the first in a series of children's stories about Stubby and his adopted son, Bobby, two midgets exploring God's great world and spreading the love of their Savior, Jesus Christ. In a collection of short chapters, these books are ideal for young

readers and short attention spans...excellent for bedtime stories.

Adventures at Mountain Haven tells about how Stubby retires from his job at a helicopter factory and takes up residence in the breathtaking mountains of the northwest. God leads him to Seattle where he discovers Bobby wandering the streets in illness, having run away from the orphanage. The adventure continues as he adopts Bobby and introduces him to his great grizzly bear friend, Silver Tip, back at Mountain Haven, his new home. Children learn respect for nature and all of God's creatures, as well as develop a grateful and loving heart. **No. 153**

African Adventures (Stubby Stories No. 2)
Lloyd Fezler
The continuing adventures of Stubby and Bobby as they explore the African wilderness. Exceptional photos of the big cats in their natural habitat make this a fascinating book for children, as well as those reading it to them. **No. 277**

More African Adventures (Stubby Stories No. 3)
Lloyd Fezler
Further adventures in the wilds of Africa, as Stubby and Bobby learn more about God's creatures and God's Plan in nature, made even more exciting by the beautiful photos of the wild animals in their native territory. **No. 279**

Covered Wagon Boy
Kermit Shelby
An adventure story in a historical setting, designed especially for the young. There is no generation gap, as Mr. Shelby captures the imagination of boys and girls when he deals realistically with the adventures that were oftentimes commonplace during the rugged pioneer days...the setting for this historical novel, where—in contrast to the violence and immorality to which we are being subjected today concerning our forefathers—we learn that the majority were God-fearing ancestors, "morals" was not a dirty word, and the term "situation ethics" had yet to be invented.

Covered Wagon Boy relates the adventures of Thad and Bright Water. Nothing could turn youngsters into adults faster than a year on the wagon trail west! Life was exciting in a wagon train...sometimes dangerous...sometimes funny...but seldom dull as the many different lives blended into one interdependent community—almost an overgrown family—with everything from marryin' to buryin'. Thad and Bright Water became lifelong friends, as did many others because of the year they shared. **No. 124**

ORIGINS SERIES

Dinosaur ABC's (K-2)
A book that every child and teacher will enjoy. This is a carefully documented, origins-balanced treatment of dinosaurs. **No. 048, Paper; No. 049, Cloth;** Teacher's Guide **No. 514**

Walk The Dinosaur Trail (3-4)
A unique approach that takes the reader into an intimate understanding of the dinosaur world and what it might have been like. This module is reading level controlled and vocabulary development oriented. The teacher's guide has many helps that every teacher will want. **No. 181;** Teacher's Guide **No. 517**

Hummy and the Wax Castle (4-6)
Little Hummy tells Josh all about his honey-making activities. Josh thanks God for creating Hummy. Children will learn much from Hummy's story. **No. 085**

Fossils, Frogs, Fish, and Friends (4-6)
The story of the fossils is discussed by two students, Chris and Evy. Chris shows why the scientific data point to a great flood that covered the earth. (For Christian schools.) **No. 156**

Voyage Through Interplanetary Space (5-7)
An exciting trip to all of the planets gives the readers new and interesting information about God's creation. **No. 176**

Fossils: Hard Facts From the Earth (5-8)
This book brings a well-documented and realistic approach to the fossil record. Every student will enjoy exploring the fossil record with Evy and Chris. **No. 064;** Teacher's Guide **No. 516**

The Eye, A Light Receiver (5-7)
A descriptive analysis of the structure and function of the human eye. The development of the eye is explored in an open-ended manner regarding origins. **No. 060;** Teacher's Guide **No. 515**

Bomby, The Bombardier Beetle (4-6)
A story about the bombardier beetle. Little Bomby learns about where he came from and how his cannons work. No reader will want to miss his story. (For Christian school.) **No. 031**

GOD IN CREATION SERIES
These beautifully illustrated full-color booklets explain to children—on a level and in terms they can full comprehend—the miracles of God's creation in 10 different scientific areas. As the titles reveal, the emphasis is on *God's Plan* for His creations and all nature supports the fact that behind everything there is a great plan. . and a Great Planner.

God's Plan for Air, No. 191
God's Plan for Animals, No. 192
God's Plan for Birds, No. 193
God's Plan for Insects, No. 194
God's Plan for Me, No. 195
God's Plan for Plants, No. 196
God's Plan for The Seashore, No. 197
God's Plan for Seasons, No. 198
God's Plan for Seeds, No. 199
God's Plan for Weather, No. 200

GOD'S WORLD SERIES from A Beka Book
This popular science series features Biblically and scientifically sound material geared to the comprehension level of elementary and junior high children. Its basic goal is to develop an appreciation of God as the Master Designer and nature as His world which can be understood and enjoyed. All books are beautifully illustrated in full color.

K - God's World, ages 4-6, 8½'' x 11'', **No. 016**
1 - Discovering God's World, ages 5-7, 8½'' x 11'', **No. 017**
2 - Enjoying God's World, ages 6-8, 8½'' x 11'', **No. 018**
3 - Exploring God's World, ages 7-9, 8½'' x 11'', **No. 019**
4 - Understanding God's World, ages 8-10, 7¼'' x 9'', **No. 020**
5 - Investigating God's World, ages 9-11, 7¼'' x 9'', **No. 021**
6 - Observing God's World, ages 10-12, 7¼'' x 9'', **No. 022**
7 - Science: Order & Reality, ages 11-13, 7¼'' x 9'', **No. 024**
8 - Science: Matter in Motion, ages 12-14, 7¼'' x 9'', **No. 029**
9 - Science of Physical Creation, ages 13-15, 7¼'' x 9'', **No. 336**